OECD Reviews on Local Job Creation

Preparing the Basque Country, Spain for the Future of Work

This document, as well as any data and map included herein, are without prejudice to the status of or sovereignty over any territory, to the delimitation of international frontiers and boundaries and to the name of any territory, city or area.

Please cite this publication as:
OECD (2020), *Preparing the Basque Country, Spain for the Future of Work*, OECD Reviews on Local Job Creation, OECD Publishing, Paris, *https://doi.org/10.1787/86616269-en*.

ISBN 978-92-64-36400-4 (print)
ISBN 978-92-64-38696-9 (pdf)

OECD Reviews on Local Job Creation
ISSN 2311-2328 (print)
ISSN 2311-2336 (online)

Photo credits: Cover © LucVi/Gettyimages.com.

Corrigenda to publications may be found on line at: *www.oecd.org/about/publishing/corrigenda.htm*.
© OECD 2020

The use of this work, whether digital or print, is governed by the Terms and Conditions to be found at *http://www.oecd.org/termsandconditions*.

Foreword

COVID-19 is testing the Basque Country's resilience. In the spring of 2020, the region had a large number of cases and implemented strong measures to help contain the virus, including a confinement of the population, and a halt to non-essential economic activity. The Basque government put in place a host of measures to strengthen the health system while also supporting individuals and firms to cope with the labour market shock.

Economic crisis often leads to profound changes in the way people live and work. COVID-19 is likely to accelerate structural changes in the labour market, including automation and digitalisation. Firms may increasingly look to technology as a way to pandemic proof their operations, while individuals may develop preferences for automated services as opposed to face-to-face contact. This OECD report sheds light on the potential impacts of automation on the Basque labour market, including which types of jobs and groups of workers are most likely to be impacted. The report also highlights the critical role to be played by employment services and training policies to help people and firms make better labour market transitions into emerging job opportunities. The Basque Country's robust employment and skills system is at the frontline of the crisis response.

This report is part of the Programme of Work of the OECD Local Economic and Employment Development (LEED) Programme. Created in 1982, the LEED Programme aims to contribute to the creation of more and better jobs in more productive and inclusive economies. It produces guidance to make the implementation of national policies more effective at the local level, while stimulating innovative practices on the ground. The OECD LEED Directing Committee, which gathers governments of OECD member and non-member countries, oversees the work of the LEED Programme.

Acknowledgements

This report has been prepared by the OECD Centre for Entrepreneurship, SMEs, Regions and Cities (CFE), led by Lamia Kamal-Chaoui, Director. This work was conducted as part of the OECD's Local Economic and Employment Development (LEED) Programme with financial support from the government of the Basque Country (Spain).

The primary authors of this report are Lucas Leblanc, Policy Analyst CFE/LESI Division and Miguel Peromingo, Employment Policy Consultant under the supervision of Jonathan Barr, Deputy Head of the CFE/LESI Division and Head of the Employment and Skills Unit, who also drafted sections of the report and coordinated the overall project. Karen Maguire, Head of the CFE/LESI Division, provided overall guidance and feedback on the development of the report. Ida Peltonen, from CFE/LESI provided statistical support to the report under the supervision of Alexander Lembcke, Economist, CFE/ESG. OECD colleagues within the Directorate for Employment, Labour and Social Affairs (ELS) provided helpful comments on a draft version of this report, including Glenda Quintini, Thedora Xenogiani, Anne Lauringson, and Katharine Mullock.

Basque government officials, at the time of drafting, played an instrumental role in the co-ordination of this project, and provided constructive feedback on the development of the report. In particular, the OECD would like to thank Javier Ramos Salazar, Head of the Lanbide technical cabinet, Maria Jalon Del Rio, Lanbide, Amaia Arteaga Dañobeitia, former Director of Employment and Inclusion in the Department of Employment and Marcos Muro Nájera, former Deputy Minister of Employment and Youth in the Basque government.

The OECD would like to express its gratitude to the Department of Employment and the Department of Education for their input in various parts of this project. Rikardo Lamadrid Intxaurraga, Director of Technology and Advanced Learning, Tknika, Basque Department of Education and Tknika staff provided key information about the functioning of vocational training in the Basque Country. The OECD would also like to thank Susana Franco and Mercedes Oleaga of Orkestra, the Basque Institute for Competitiveness, for their input on the report. The OECD would also like to thank Michael Stein, Area Manager in the regional directorate of North Rhine-Westphalia of the German employment services, and Gunn-Elin Åsgren, Product Manager, Norwegian Labour and Welfare Administration, for sharing their experience in public employment services with counterparts in the Basque Country.

Finally, the OECD would like to thank all local representatives that participated in the OECD's fact-finding mission and workshops. These include representatives from Confebask, the Unión General de Trabajadores (UGT), Comisiones Obreras (CCOO), the Asociación empresarial de sociedades laborales y empresas participadas de la Comunidad Autónoma del País Vasco (ASLE), the Confederación de Cooperativas de Euskadi (KONFEKOOP), the chambers of commerce of Alava, Bilbao and Gipuzoka, the Asociación de mujeres empresarias, Garapen, the Consejo de la juventud de Euskadi, Novia Salcedo, the Universidad del País Vasco / Euskal Herriko Unibertsitatea (UPV/EHU), the Univerisdad de Deusto, Mondragon Unibertsitatea, the Asociación de Entidades de Trabajo Protegido del País Vasco (ELHABE), the Asociación de Empresas de Inserción del País Vasco (GIZATEA), Lanbide and the Basque government.

Table of contents

Foreword 3

Acknowledgements 4

Acronyms and Abbreviations 8

Executive Summary 10

1. Assessment and recommendations 13
   The future of work in the Basque Country (Spain) 13
   Lanbide can reinforce its role as a labour market actor in the face of COVID-19 16
   Mobilising skills in the Basque Country 18

2. The effects of automation in the Basque Country, Spain 21
   Introduction 23
   2.1. COVID-19 will have unequal impacts on workers, firms and places 23
   2.2. What will be the impacts of automation in the Basque Country? 29
   2.3. Job quality: a "high road" recovery can prepare the Basque Country for the future of work 42
   Conclusion 47
   References 48

3. Designing responsive employment services to help people into good jobs 51
   Introduction 53
   3.1. Lanbide has developed its capacities significantly to face the future of work 53
   3.2. Opportunities for Lanbide in the new world of work 60
   Conclusion 73
   References 74
   Notes 75

4. Skills in the Basque Country 77
   Introduction 79
   4.1. The Basque workforce's high skills are an opportunity for the region 79
   4.2. The Basque Vocation educational and training system 94
   Conclusion 100
   References 101

Tables

Table 1.1. Many industrial jobs could be automated, posing both threats and opportunities for the Basque Country — 14
Table 2.1. Automation bottlenecks — 32
Table 2.2. Industrial jobs in the Basque Country are at particular risk of destruction or change due to automation — 35
Table 2.3 Automatable service-associated jobs are common in sectors at risk from COVID-19 — 37
Table 3.1. Outside of the unemployed, young people and women are the focus of many Lanbide employment programmes — 58
Table 3.2. Lanbide services reach both employed and unemployment people in the labour market — 58
Table 3.3. Examples of how other OECD countries manage active and passive labour market policies — 71

Figures

Figure 2.1. Employment-support measures are helping limit surges in unemployment in the Basque Country, though the crisis has reversed years of recovery — 24
Figure 2.2. The Basque Country is well positioned for teleworking among Spanish regions — 25
Figure 2.3. The 2008 crisis hit employment hardest in the construction and industrial sectors — 26
Figure 2.4. Productivity increases struggled to accompany employment growth following the 2008 crisis — 27
Figure 2.5. Employment in industrial manufacturing, food services and accommodation showed the greatest signs of distress — 28
Figure 2.6. OECD calculations show trade-related employment at particularly high risk in the Basque Country — 29
Figure 2.7. More jobs in the Basque Country are high risk compared to the OECD average, though less than all other regions in Spain — 31
Figure 2.8. Men and immigrants tend to occupy jobs with tasks more likely to be automated — 33
Figure 2.9. Automation may accelerate losses in industrial employment — 35
Figure 2.10. The Basque Country has shed high skill occupations at lower risk of automation — 39
Figure 2.11. Futurelan is a helpful tool to evaluate occupational change of the future in the Basque Country — 41
Figure 2.12. The share of temporary workers is well above the EU average in Spain, and has been on an upward trajectory — 44
Figure 2.13. Part-time contracts are pervasive in the Basque Country — 46
Figure 2.14. Involuntary part-time employment makes up the majority of part-time work in Spain — 46
Figure 3.1. The Basque Country devotes a similar amount of financial resources to labour market policies as west European countries — 55
Figure 3.2. Lanbide ranks among the top in registering unemployed jobseekers compared to all available OECD averages, 2018 — 56
Figure 3.3. Since taking over responsibilities for employment services, Lanbide also registers a high proportion of long term unemployed people — 57
Figure 3.4. Lanbide programmes are reaching an increasing number of young people — 59
Figure 3.5. Unemployed people do not declare Lanbide as a leading job search means — 62
Figure 3.6. Service levels for jobseekers at Lanbide — 64
Figure 3.7. Initial jobseeker streaming in employment services Australia — 65
Figure 3.8. The number of RGI claimants has also been decreasing with the recovery — 67
Figure 3.9. The amount of funds devoted to RGI has been decreasing since 2018 — 67
Figure 3.10. Few RGI recipients find quality jobs on the labour market — 68
Figure 3.11. Lanbide staff handle a relatively high number of caseloads per staff member, as much of their time is devoted to administering RGI claims — 69
Figure 3.12. Long-term unemployed people risk losing benefits and activation measures — 70
Figure 3.13. There is room for more jobseekers to benefit from Lanbide labour market insertion programmes — 70
Figure 4.1. Middle-skilled jobs have declined since 2000 — 80
Figure 4.2. Educational attainment has progressed steadily in the Basque Country — 81
Figure 4.3. The Basque Country has been successful at moving towards a highly educated workforce — 81
Figure 4.4. The dependency ratio has risen considerably since 2011 — 82
Figure 4.5. Many Basque workers are in occupations under their skill level — 83
Figure 4.6. Some firms declare difficulties hiring — 85
Figure 4.7. Firm response suggest job quality is a leading reason for the mismatch — 85
Figure 4.8. Adult learning participation is slightly below the Spanish and OECD average — 89
Figure 4.9. Work-place responsibilities are a leading reason for non-participation in adult learning — 91

Figure 4.10. SMEs tend to train less of their employees than large firms, but large Basque firms fall short of the Spanish average 91
Figure 4.11. Since 2011, Lanbide has developed a volley of VETE programmes to support adult learning in the region 94
Figure 4.12. VET enrolment has been rising in the Basque Country since 2011, though women make up a small share of students 96
Figure 4.13. Mechanical production and IT and communications led enrolment in 2019 96

Boxes

Box 1.1. Recommendations to future-proof the Basque Country through skills foresight 15
Box 1.2. Recommendations to reinforce Lanbide's role as a labour market actor 17
Box 1.3. Recommendations to encourage firms to better use skills and create quality jobs in the Basque Country 19
Box 2.1. COVID-19 is likely to accelerate the uptake of labour-saving technologies 30
Box 2.2. How does the OECD calculate the risk of job automation? 32
Box 2.3. Basque industrial reconversion in 1980-1990 34
Box 2.4. International good practice: Supporting mid-career workers in the industrial sector in Ontario, Canada 36
Box 2.5. Finding synergies between local skills and specialisation strategies 40
Box 2.6. International good practice: Industry skills mapping in Wallonia (Belgium) 42
Box 2.7. The *Plan director por un trabajo digno 2018-2020*: the Spanish government's strategy to reduce precarious work 45
Box 2.8. "High road" firm strategies to support job quality and productivity 47
Box 3.1. How are employment services across the OECD responding to COVID-19? 54
Box 3.2. How do other OECD employment services approach general versus specialised supports 61
Box 3.3. Lanbide can expand its role in a changing world of work 63
Box 3.4. Digital first at the Flemish public employment service 65
Box 3.5. Building strong employer engagement through reverse marketing in Australia 72
Box 4.1. How local actors mobilised to change work practices in the Rivera del Brenta industrial district in Italy 84
Box 4.2. A government employer survey of firms can reinforce information on skills needs and use 86
Box 4.3. In Sweden, Job Security Councils support workers through transition 88
Box 4.4. Workplace innovation in Scotland 90
Box 4.5. Promoting SME networks and enterprise-led learning: The example of Skillnet, Ireland 92
Box 4.6. Individual training accounts as a response to the future of work 93
Box 4.7. Understanding VET as life-long learning in France and Finland 97
Box 4.8. Tknika, the Basque Centre for Applied Innovation in Vocational Training 98
Box 4.9. Individual, co-drafted apprenticeship plans in Slovenia 100

Acronyms and Abbreviations

ACRiB	*Associazione Calzaturifici della Riviera del Brenta*
ALMP	Active labour market policy
AI	Artificial Intelligence
BA	*Bundesagentur für Arbeit*
CC OO	*Confederacion Sindical de Comisiones Obreras*
CON	*Clasificación Nacional de Ocupaciones*
CONFEBASK	*Confederación Empresarial Vasca*
COVID-19	Coronavirus Disease 2019
EU	European Union
ELA-STV	*Eusko Langileen Alkartasuna-Solidaridad de los Trabajadores Vascos*
ERTE	*Expedientes de regulación temporal de empleo*
EURES	European Employment Services
ESCO	European Standard Classification of Occupations
ESS	UK Employer Skills Survey
EVADES	*Evaluación de los Desempeños de los Servicios Públicos de Empleo españoles*
FO	Frey and Osborne
GDP	Gross Domestic Product
HPWP	High Performance Work Practices
JRC	European Commission Joint Research Centre
ICT	Information and Communication Technology
ILO	International Labour Organization
ISCO	International Standard Classification of Occupations
NAV	*Arbeids- og velferdseta*
OECD	Organisation for Economic Co-operation and Development
PES	Public Employment Service
PIACC	Programme for the International Assessment of Adult Competencies
RGI	*Renta Garantía Ingresos*

RIS3	Research and innovation strategies for smart specialisation
SEPE	*Servicio Público de Empleo Estatal*
SFC	SkillsFuture Credit
SME	Small and Medium-sized Enterprise
STW	Short Time Work
UGT	Sindicato Unión General de Trabajadores
VDAB	*Vlaamse Dienst voor Arbeidsbemiddeling en Beroepsopleiding*
VET	Vocational Education and Training
VETE	Vocational Education and Training for Employment

Executive Summary

The COVID-19 crisis is causing an unprecedented downturn in labour markets across the OECD. The Basque Country has been particularly affected by COVID-19, as lockdown measures in March-May 2020 ground two of its key sectors – industrial manufacturing and tourism – to a temporary halt. These parts of the economy drove requests for the Spanish government's short-term work schemes (STW) in the region.

After the 2008 economic crisis, it took over ten years to recover employment levels, while the quality of jobs suffered. Indeed, prior to COVID-19, unemployment in the Basque Country reached 9.3%, significantly lower than the Spanish average of 14.1%. COVID-19 will test the region's resilience. Unemployment sat at 13.5% as of June 2020 – an increase of 4.2 percentage points. This share is set to increase as the government phases out STW and the region faces the risk of new lockdown measures. The crisis is also likely to accentuate multiple long-term labour market shifts.

Teleworking is one of a number of structural labour market evolutions likely to take place. Around 32% of jobs can be carried out remotely in the Basque Country, a factor that can support recovery as multiple restrictions for public health remain in place. Automation is also likely to accelerate. In the Basque Country, 22% of jobs are at high risk of automation (versus 14% for the OECD), meaning they could disappear. 33% are at risk of significant change (versus the OECD average of 32%), whereby the job likely remains but the skills required to perform it change. Automation is an opportunity to raise productivity, though it also poses risks to some workers, sectors and occupations.

Basque policy actors are taking action to manage this accelerated digital transition. Lanbide, the Basque employment service, is digitalising services, enabling service continuity during COVID-19. Lanbide staff, however, would benefit from greater capacity to administer Active Labour Market Policies (ALMPs), without harming coverage of one of the region's main social policies, the Renta de Garantía de Ingresos (RGI). Social partners in the Basque Country are also moving towards a pact on a fair digital transition, which will help firms anticipate skills changes, retrain workers and avoid layoffs.

As in many OECD regions, job polarisation is occurring in the Basque Country, with middle skilled jobs declining by 6.4% since 2000. Positively, most of the shift has been towards high-skilled jobs, which grew by 4.8% versus low skilled jobs, which grew by only 1.6%. The shift to high-skilled jobs partly reflects the region's high levels of educational attainment, above Spanish and EU averages. That being said, over 33% of workers occupy jobs below their skill level. The quality of jobs has not followed the upskilling of jobs, accentuating recruitment difficulties in the region and weighing on social cohesion.

This under-utilisation of talent is a missed opportunity for the region. To mitigate this, Lanbide has taken steps to work more closely with employers. Engagement with firms to implement stronger work practices and modify job offers to better correspond to job seekers constitute new possibilities. The region's social dialogue roundtable is also setting up new labour market observatories to track change. There is also an opportunity to further encourage the upskilling of workers who are in economic sectors that will take longer to recover (or will not fully recover) or that might face structural change as a result of accelerated automation. The following recommendations could help to further enhance Basque efforts.

Future-proofing the region through better skills anticipation

- **Form an expert group composed of industry specialists to conduct skill foresight exercises across sectors and occupations**: Expert groups within Lanbide could analyse the service's rich set of data on job postings, engage with firms and formulate policy-relevant analyses of the evolution of skills demand in the region. The expert group could identify scenarios of the skills needed for different sets of occupations, expanding studies beyond the region's traditional industry base to a growing service sector. Results could be communicated to training centres for coordination and dissemination purposes.
- **Help SMEs conduct analyses of their skills needs:** A mechanism could be established to allocate funding to groups of SMEs in the same industry to conduct analyses of the skill needs they may have in common, with the goal of sharing training capacities. The Agencia vasca de desarrollo empresarial (SPRI) may be well positioned to take such a role as part of its innovation support services for Basque SMEs.
- **Put in place an employer skills survey across the Basque Country:** A publicly-administered employer survey could be established to collect information on skills challenges that employers report both within their existing workforces and when recruiting, the levels and nature of investment in training and development, and the relationship between skills challenges, training activity and business strategy. The region could take the United Kingdom as an example, where an annual employer skills survey has allowed the government to gather an idea of skills needs, training and work practices.

Reinforcing Lanbide's role as a central labour market actor

- **Lanbide's caseload can be modified to more fully implement labour market activation policies without harming coverage of passive policies:** Administration of the region's income support programme, the Renta de Garantía de Ingresos (RGI), could be streamlined and simplified. This would allow Lanbide to devote itself more fully to the delivery of activation policies – including coaching, skills training and other employment preparation programmes – as the recovery progresses.
- **Lanbide staff could help employers, and particularly SMEs, to formulate job postings based on Lanbide's job seeker information:** Dedicated teams could be established within the employment service to help design job postings based on skills identified among job seekers, while also co-creating job postings, particularly for job seekers who are ready or nearly ready to work but face barriers with advertised vacancies.
- **Build on Lanbide's *Cuenta de Formación*, or personal training account, through the greater use of data to match skills**: Building on Lanbide's recent training accounts for job seekers, programmes could connect Lanbide with training centres, helping them design programmes and evaluate training modules based on the skills of workers.

Better using the skills of the labour force and promoting quality jobs

- **Encourage firms to better use the high skills available and raise the quality of jobs:** The region can engage employers in workplace innovation strategies, such as high performance work practices (HPWP), which better use the high skills of the workforce. This could be done by setting "good practice" standards across the region that sets out guidelines on how a company can review the way it uses the skills of workers and how it designs jobs. It can also include providing direct advice to firms through intermediaries (e.g. vocational training institutions) or business networks.

- **Build new labour market tools that support worker transitions:** The Basque Country's social dialogue roundtable, the Mesa de Diálogo Social, has created new labour market observatories on skills as well as occupational health and safety. Such tools can be expanded drawing on international practices, such as Swedish job security councils, which could provide intensive personalised support to workers before job loss occurs. These could be included in the region's pact on a fair digital transition.
- **Participate in the Spanish government's labour inspection initiative to reduce the abuse of fixed-term contracts**: Coordinate through the Spanish government's *Plan director por un trabajo digno*, which has identified a large share of abusive fixed-term contracts, to focus efforts to identify labour law abuse. Sectors or occupations most at risk could be identified for the Basque labour inspectorate to co-participate in the plan's *campañas extraordinarias autonómicas*.

1. Assessment and recommendations

The future of work in the Basque Country (Spain)

The COVID-19 crisis is creating a shock in the Basque labour market, interrupting the prolonged economic recovery that has taken place since the 2008 crisis. Prior to COVID-19, unemployment had continued to decrease in the region, falling below 10% in 2019 – lower than the Spanish average of 14% but double the OECD average of around 5%. In March 2020, employment protection measures helped limit an initial surge in redundancies due to lockdown measures to limit the spread of the virus.

Although a minority of jobs can be carried out remotely, the Basque Country benefits from a relatively high share of jobs that can be carried out through telework compared to most Spanish regions. 32% of jobs can be carried out remotely compared to below 30% in most regions of Spain. Contrary to the 2008 downturn, COVID-19 puts employment in sectors linked to tourism and trade at particular risk.

The COVID-19 crisis is likely to accelerate job automation as firms may replace human labour with cost-saving robots. Already before COVID-19, automation and digitalisation where changing jobs in a number of ways. Some jobs are likely to be destroyed as technology completely replaces the need for human labour. Other jobs will significantly change in terms of the task composition required to succeed in that job. OECD estimates highlight that about 14% of jobs across OECD countries are at high risk of automation, whereas 32% are likely to significantly change going forward. For the Basque Country, those figures are higher: 22% of jobs may be at high risk of automation, with another 33% that may be at significant risk of automation. In total, this means that 205 000 jobs are at high risk of automation, with an additional 293 000 at risk of significant change.

Automation, however, presents new opportunities for the Basque Country, and the government is leveraging its tradition of industrial policy to integrate technology in its industrial base. Indeed, the region's newest industrial and innovation strategies – from an *Industria 4.0* industrialisation strategy to a Smart Specialisation Strategy (RIS3) focused on advanced manufacturing – will encourage Basque firms to integrate new technologies into their production processes to improve their competitive position.

Evidence from this OECD study reveals that middle and low skill occupations related to the region's industrial manufacturing sector are particularly at risk of automation. Among the highest risk occupations, 38 600 stationary plant and machine operator positions are at high and significant risk, along with 37 900 metal, machinery and related trades workers and 32 700 drivers and mobile plant operators (Table 1.1). Multiple service occupations are also at high or significant risk. In particular, these include low and middle skill jobs involving routine tasks such as cleaning or washing, cleaners and helpers, personal care workers and sales workers, representing respectively 42 000, 25 400 and 36 000 jobs. Given the need for increasing sanitary measures, there could be an accelerated use of robots within these occupational categories to mitigate health risks.

Table 1.1. Many industrial jobs could be automated, posing both threats and opportunities for the Basque Country

Top 10 occupations with greater number of people with jobs at high risk of automation in the Basque Country, 2018

Occupation	Number of people at high risk	High risk, %	Number of people at significant risk,	Risk of significant change, %	Total employed people at risk of automation
Stationary Plant and Machine Operators	23 200	48	15 400	32	38 600
Metal, Machinery and Related Trades Workers	19 700	31	18 200	28	37 900
Drivers and Mobile Plant Operators	17 500	45	15 200	39	32 700
Cleaners and Helpers	15 100	32	26 900	56	42 000
Personal Care Workers	14 000	39	11 400	32	25 400
Sales Workers	11 700	17	24 300	34	36 000
Personal Service Workers	11 500	25	17 000	37	28 500
Numerical and Material Recording Clerks	10 400	31	9 700	29	20 100
Assemblers	8 400	44	10 500	56	18 900
Building and Related Trades Workers (excluding Electricians	23 200	48	15 400	32	16 700

Note: The 100% estimate for Assemblers is due to statistical uncertainty. High rates of automation for this occupation correspond to prior OECD research.
Source: OECD calculations based on the European Labour Force Survey.

The adoption of new technologies in the workplace has paralleled job losses in the region's manufacturing industry. The industrial sector lost 64 000 jobs between 2008 and 2015, before recovering partly in the years prior to COVID-19. Between 2008 and 2018, the Basque Country tended to create jobs in occupations both at high and low risk of automation. The region created over 12 300 stationary plant and machine operator positions and over 19 000 metal, machinery and related trades workers since 2008, occupations at high risk of automation. The Basque Country, meanwhile, lost 20 300 cleaners and helper positions and 23 800 building and related trades workers. Worker re-training for high risk occupations can be levered into an opportunity to raise labour productivity hand-in-hand with social cohesion.

After the 2008 crisis, the region also tended to lose high-skill service-related jobs at lower risk of automation, such as business and administration associate professionals, business and administration professionals and legal, social and cultural professionals, losing approximately 14 800, 7 500 and 840 jobs respectively. These losses indicate the region may be struggling to move into higher skilled occupations that may be more resilient to automation outside of its industrial base. This may also constitute a missed opportunity given the region's high level of educational attainment.

The quality of employment has also decreased in the Basque Country. As in the rest of Spain, involuntary part-time work and temporary contracts have grown, while wages for many groups have stagnated. Indeed, 92% of contracts signed in 2019 in the region were temporary. Meanwhile, the number of people working but at risk of poverty rose in Spain throughout the recovery, suggesting that a share of new jobs may not pay a living wage. These trends have particularly degraded the working conditions of lower skilled workers. At the national level, the Spanish government put in place the *Plan director por un trabajo digno,* a policy involving labour inspections and big data to curb the abuse of temporary, part-time and precarious contracts.

The Basque Country has multiple assets it can mobilise to face the risks associated with the future of work, particularly as an integrated part of its recovery plan from the COVID-19 crisis. In particular, the region's public employment service, Lanbide, has developed a volley of tools to collect data on skills developments. Leaning on its world-renowned experience with industry clusters and industrial policy, the Basque Country has also developed a volley of strategic plans to steer the way innovation and technology enters production. These experiences set the base for new strategies to engage with employers on innovative workplace strategies that use the region's high skills as a driver for an inclusive recovery.

> **Box 1.1. Recommendations to future-proof the Basque Country through skills foresight**
>
> **Use Lanbide's rich information on the evolution of occupations to map skills**
>
> - **Form an expert group composed of industry specialists to build on skills mapping and foresight exercises of key sectors and occupations.** Lanbide could build on its quantitative analytical tools, such as Futurelan, to engage in a large scale occupational mapping exercise to predict skills evolutions in the region. Lanbide could turn to examples from Wallonia (Belgium) and Ireland, where the public employment services form expert groups according to specific sectors to analyse occupational data and formulate policy-oriented recommendations related to skills and training. Lanbide could create an industry expert group which could identify potential scenarios for occupations within the region, while also meeting regularly to evaluate labour market changes. Results can be communicated directly to relevant stakeholders, such as training centres, unions and industry groups.
>
> **Helping companies better identify their own skills needs, driving lifelong learning priorities**
>
> - **Put in place an employer skills survey across the Basque Country**. A government-administered employer survey can include information on skills challenges that employers report both within their existing workforces and when recruiting, the levels and nature of investment in training and development, and the relationship between skills challenges, training activity and business strategy. The region could build on a skills study performed by Confebask, the employer federation, while addressing the study to a larger groups of firms and a greater array of questions.
>
> - **Help SMEs conduct analyses of their skills needs**. For instance, a mechanism could allocate funding to groups of businesses in the same industry sector or with similar training needs in order to deliver subsidised training. Such a programme enables firms to respond to changing skills demands through both formal and informal learning. Such a programme is well suited to connect with the region's industry clusters, where firms and public bodies maintain an ongoing dialogue on regional competitiveness strategies.

Lanbide can reinforce its role as a labour market actor in the face of COVID-19

The Basque public employment service (PES), Lanbide, has adopted its services in light of COVID-19 by prioritising social needs arising from the crisis. Lanbide provided income supplements to recipients of temporary unemployment benefits, while it also began administering the *Ingreso Minimo Vital*, a minimum social revenue launched by the Spanish government during the lockdown. Lanbide's crisis role is an opportunity to tailor its policies to the recovery, as new cohorts of unemployed people enter its programmes, and the PES is faced with a digitalising labour market.

Across the OECD, the role of new technologies in job searches, labour market transitions and work itself is raising challenges. Automation is supressing and changing the skills required to work in certain occupations, calling for employment services to handle more complex job transitions. Digitalisation, meanwhile, is facilitating the development of new forms of work, such as platform and remote work. Indeed, in 2019, the Basque government introduced a bill with points aiming to reinforce Lanbide's digital services to adapt to these changes (*Anteproyecto de Ley/2019 del Sistema Vasco de Empleo y de* Lanbide-*Servicio Vasco de Empleo*).

Lanbide is a critical actor to support the recovery from COVID-19. The Basque Country's spending on labour market policies represents around 1.3 % of its GDP, a similar proportion to countries such as Germany, Italy and Denmark. Specifically, the Basque Country spends approximately 41% of its labour market public spending on active labour market measures, while 59% is spent on benefits and other supports. Spending on Lanbide programmes nearly halved between 2012 and 2013 before recovering, which may have harmed their delivery during crisis.

Lanbide has grown its staff from 550 employed full time equivalents in 2011 to 920 in 2019 to support its expanding role. Lanbide's strategy consists of providing a generalist mentor service, which registers job seekers and navigates them through employment and activation possibilities. This allows for strong initial support, before turning to Lanbide's specialised entities and partners to guide job seekers into training or other services. Lanbide administers 65 activation and job stimulation measures, such as work practices or employer incentives. Most programmes in 2019 were targeted on the inclusion of young people and women, with 11 programmes for each target group. This attention on youth and women will help Lanbide as new cohorts of young people and women, who tend to suffer from precarious contracts, bear the brunt of the COVID-19 downturn.

Lanbide is responsible for administering and disbursing the welfare benefit *Renta de Garantia de Ingresos* (RGI) which provides income assistance to individuals and families in need. It also aims to help those able to work into employment. In 2019, Lanbide administered EUR 489 million in RGI to more than 52 000 people. In 2018, RGI recipients received 42% of the vocational guidance service offered as part of Lanbide services to job seekers and took part in 17% of the offered trainings. Through RGI, Lanbide will be able to provide a strong safety net as the region faces the ongoing consequences of the COVID-19 crisis.

The RGI is a pillar of the Basque welfare system and a local strength in a changing world of work: the guaranteed income measure has helped reduce poverty in the region and its links with activation measures have helped accompany people into training. Nonetheless, more job seekers could benefit from job activation measures. For instance, only 23% of RGI recipients able to work were assisted into jobs in 2019. This may be due to Lanbide's high caseload of RGI recipients, which Lanbide management estimate requires four times as much time as a non-RGI case. Using this estimate, Lanbide activation staff have 427 cases per staff member, a high caseload compared to OECD countries dedicating comparable budgets on PES. This caseload proportion may prevent staff from devoting sufficient time to activation, as well as other passive measures, causing non take-up of policies. Indeed, the PES is only used as a mediator to offer or find jobs by between 30% to 48 % of jobseekers unemployed for less than six months, and by between 33% to 50% of long-term unemployed in the region.

To mitigate low outreach, the reform bill for employment services includes the possibility of integrating a greater number of labour market agencies in Lanbide's programmes to lighten responsibilities related to RGI, while also furthering Lanbide's digital strategy. Indeed, in multiple OECD countries, PES are using digital tools to track and guide their clients' careers and be able to connect to databases of other partners like training institutes or social workers from other parts of government.

Close work with employers may help Lanbide administer labour market policies more effectively. Services to employers are given a high strategic priority within Lanbide in order to create perspectives for future labour market developments. To better connect labour market needs with job seekers, vocational education and training can offer more short-term trainings directly linked to concrete job or skills, a role that can be facilitated by a PES. Lanbide is also taking major steps to improve accreditation of skills and experiences, although more could be done to recognise transversal and soft skills and increase job readiness, particularly for low skill job seekers.

Box 1.2. Recommendations to reinforce Lanbide's role as a labour market actor

Reinforcing Lanbide staff capacity to administer both active and passive policies

- **Lanbide's caseload can be modified to allow it to more fully implement activation without harming coverage of RGI, a pillar of social cohesion in the region.** As Lanbide is likely to face a rising number of RGI applications as the social consequences of COVID-19 are felt, accelerating RGI applications by streamlining administrative procedures could help manage a growing caseload. Reducing time devoted to RGI can improve staff capacity to administer Lanbide's host of active programmes.

Helping firms conceive jobs according to job seekers skills

- **Lanbide staff can help employers, and particularly SMEs, to formulate job postings based on Lanbide's job seeker information.** This could include dedicated teams to design job postings based on the skills identified among job seekers, while also reaching out to prospective employers who may not be aware of Lanbide's skills pool. Lanbide could use this as a way to co-create job postings. For employers, especially SMEs with less human resource capacity, Lanbide's help in job offer design can help these firms be best aware of the skills of current job seekers, helping to reduce hiring difficulties. For job seekers, particularly those who are ready or nearly ready to work but face barriers with advertised vacancies, the co-creation of vacancies can reduce barriers into employment.

Connecting personal training accounts with training centres

- **Lanbide can build on its Cuenta de Formación, or personal training accounts for job seekers, to create digitally connected training programmes.** Such programmes could connect data on Lanbide users with training centres, helping training centres design programmes and evaluate training modules around the skills and preferences of job seekers. Training accounts, such as the Cuenta de Formación, for individual job seekers could support such digitally connected training programmes. Appropriate data protection also needs to be included.

Mobilising skills in the Basque Country

The recovery from the COVID-19 crisis is an opportunity to better use skills in the region. The skills demanded by jobs are changing in the Basque Country. Job polarisation has accelerated in the region since the 2008 crisis. Middle skill jobs have decreased by over 6.4 percentage points, while low skill and high skill grew by 1.6 and 4.8 percentage points respectively since 2000, following general trends in Spain. Automation is likely to drive middle skill job loss in the region, while changes in wage-setting may have contributed to the creation of low skill jobs. Most of these middle-skill jobs are shifting into high-skill job creation, though pay and working conditions are not keeping pace.

Upskilling also reflects the Basque workforces high educational attainment rates relative to the OECD and Spanish averages. The share of the Basque population with tertiary education has grown steadily in the last two decades, increasing from 32% in 2000 to nearly 50% of the population in 2018.

A survey by Confebask, the Basque employer federation, notes that firms in the region declare difficulties hiring. According to this survey, 48% of Basque companies surveyed declared difficulties hiring in 2016, a number that rose to 71% in 2018. Although this suggests a degree of skills mismatch, it also reflects low job quality, as the region's highly educated workforce may not find jobs that utilises its skills, allows for career development and provides attractive wages and working conditions.

Indeed, 33.5% of people are over-qualified for their job in the Basque Country versus 16.8% across the OECD and 14.7% in the EU. Confebask firms surveyed declared lack of training/specialisation and lack of experience, along with lack of interest and wages, as the top reasons for hiring difficulties. In this way, there is a greater role for both companies to better adapt to the high level of skills of Basque workers and for the training and activation policies to better articulate with job demand. In the same vein, Basque planning strategies could help stimulate job creation in jobs requiring the higher level qualifications of the workforce. This could include stimulating job creation in higher-skill service jobs.

The region's renewed social dialogue round table, the *Mesa de Diálogo Social,* can support workers to adapt their skills and for firms to strengthen the quality of jobs. In particular, the region is moving towards a social pact for the future of work, including an agreement to prevent layoffs due to automation by anticipating skills needs. The roundtable is also creating new labour market initiatives, such as labour market observatories for occupational health and safety or skills. Such joint initiatives between employer and worker representatives lay the basis for new labour market tools to drive an inclusive digital transition.

Adult learning also constitutes a growing opportunity to support workers adapt skills and for firms to strengthen the quality of jobs. As COVID-19 causes an unprecedented shock to the region's labour market while causing durable downturns in certain sectors and occupations, adult learning can be a key way to ensure workers integrate new skills. Prior to COVID-19, under 21% of SME employees received training in the Basque Country, while over 39% of workers in larger firms can benefit from training.

In this way, the region can bring to bear important strengths, ranging from Lanbide's array of labour market policies, to a Vocational Education and Training (VET) system of excellence. Indeed, the region's vocational training institutions benefit from a high profile within the Department of Education, and can lean on close links with the region's enterprises and innovation strategy. For instance, the Tknika centre, tied to the VET Department, connects vocational training centres to Basque firms and universities to help centres adopt applied research and innovation. The region's VET has also emphasised ties with employers and brought forth more opportunities for international exchange. As part of this proximity to employers, the region's VET system has increased the use of dual education, helping many Basque students integrate the labour market following training.

Employers can play a leadership role in this change in training culture and skills use in the Basque Country. Meanwhile, other actors in the region can help accompany and incite companies to strengthen their work practices. As most firms in the Basque Country are SMEs with less human resource capacities, they may struggle to define their skills needs and best use the competences of their employees. Research suggests that employers that innovate in their work organisation – by using strategies such as High Performance Work Practices (HPWP) –can improve productivity while supporting job satisfaction. Improving access to training in the workplace can be an important element of a competitiveness and job quality strategy.

> Box 1.3. Recommendations to encourage firms to better use skills and create quality jobs in the Basque Country
>
> **Encouraging firms to better use skills and invest in the quality of jobs**
>
> - **Encourage firms to adopt "high road" strategies based on workforce training and job quality.** As part of a broad strategy, the government could use its "Basque Industry 4.0" industrial strategy to provide specific funds to firms that adopt digitalisation hand-in-hand with business strategies focused on workforce engagement. As recovery from COVID-19 begins, "good practice" standards could incite companies to follow fair practices, such as decent pay and adult learning, that also encourage companies to move into higher value added products or services. The Basque Country's historic industry clusters are an asset to encourage new firm strategies, as they could encourage companies to pool resources for training or formulate common marketing strategies.
> - **Monitor the abuse of fixed-term contracts to raise the quality of jobs.** The region's Department of Employment and Social Policies, along with the *Inspección de Trabajo*, the Basque Labour inspectorate, could engage in a regional complement to the Spanish government's *Plan Director por un Trabajo Digno 2018-2020*, or strategy for dignified work. For example, the central government's plan includes structures for regional-national collaboration, such as *campañas extraordinarias autonómicas*, or the possibility for tailored regional additions to the plan. As part of this plan, social partners and other government departments could be invited to contribute to planning. Sectors or occupations most at risk could be identified, while public communications can make clear that only enterprises that abuse labour law are concerned.
>
> **Using social dialogue for an inclusive future of work**
>
> - **Promote a social dialogue agreement on the COVID-19 recovery.** The Pacto Social Vasco para una Transición justa a la Industria 4.0, or the pact for a just 4.0 industrial transition, can help ensure job losses are anticipated and mitigated through training and social support. Based on this pact, an agreement on the principles for the economic recovery could mitigate job losses and sustain job quality, while ensuring companies can adjust to new conditions.
> - **Build new labour market institutions that support worker transitions.** New tools, such as job security councils, could work in tandem with labour market observatories to anticipate job losses. Such institutions could work with Lanbide to link workers with retraining programmes and income support based on intensive personal counselling.

2. The effects of automation in the Basque Country, Spain

This chapter analyses the future of work in the Basque Country, Spain. The COVID-19 crisis has resulted in a labour market shock, reversing years of progressive job growth. COVID-19 is likely to accelerate automation in the region as firms look to technology as a way to pandemic proof their operations. Automation could put some jobs at-risk, including within the region's historical industrial base. COVID-19 may also accelerate the automation of certain service-based occupations, such as sales workers or cleaning staff. The region, however, is in a strong position for this transition, as it benefits from a high share of jobs that can be carried out remotely, while Lanbide, the region's public employment service, is taking steps to map the way occupations are evolving.

In Brief

The COVID-19 crisis is likely to accelerate automation in the Basque Country

- The COVID-19 crisis will cause an unprecedented downturn in the Basque labour market, interrupting the prolonged recovery in employment since the 2008 crisis. Prior to COVID-19, unemployment had continued to decrease in the region, falling below 10% in 2019 – lower than the Spanish average of 14% but double the OECD average of around 5%. Employment protection measures put in place by the Spanish and Basque governments helped limit an initial surge in redundancies due to lockdown measures. The majority of requests for Short Time Work (STW) schemes came from industrial manufacturing and food services and accommodation, totalling 33.1% and 19.1% of all requests respectively (10 June 2020).

- The Basque Country benefits from a relatively high share of jobs that can be carried out remotely compared to most Spanish regions, with 32% of jobs that can be carried out remotely, leaving 68% without the possibility of teleworking.

- The COVID-19 crisis is likely to accelerate job automation in the region. Prior to the crisis, over 205 000 and 293 000 jobs were calculated to be at high or significant risk of automation respectively, representing 22% and 32% of employment in the Basque Country. The OECD calculates that a job is at high risk if over 70% of tasks within an occupation are likely to be automated, while ones at significant risk is where 50-70% of tasks could be automated, requiring workers to reskill.

- Between 2008 and 2017, job loss in the Basque Country was concentrated in the region's manufacturing and construction sectors. The region lost 50 300 construction jobs and 51 300 in industrial manufacturing, representing respective falls of 5 and 2.47 percentage points of total employment. Contrary to these trends, the COVID-19 crisis is likely to drive job loss and creation in sectors particularly linked to tourism and trade. Discounting employment protection measures, OECD calculations predict 10% of employment in retail and wholesale trade in the Basque Country to be at risk of suppression, compared to 12.4% in Catalonia and 10.9% in Madrid.

- Within sectoral trends, the Basque Country tended to create jobs in occupations both at high and low risk of automation between 2008 and 2018. The region created over 12 300 stationary plant and machine operator positions and over 19 000 metal, machinery and related trades workers since 2008, occupations at high risk of automation. Meanwhile, the Basque Country lost 20 300 cleaners and helper positions and 23 800 building and related trades workers, also at high risk of automation.

- Raising job quality is an opportunity to strengthen resilience and drive recovery in the Basque Country. However, following Spanish averages, temporary and involuntary part-time employment has proliferated in the Basque Country, with many contracts lasting less than six months, or even one week. In 2019, 92% of contracts signed in the Basque Country had a defined end date, while the OECD has ranked Spain among the lowest countries on job quality. Skill utilisation strategies offer an opportunity for the region to incite companies to invest in employee skills and move firms into higher value added products.

Introduction

Automation and digitalisation are likely to accelerate as the *Comunidad Autónoma del País Vasco* in Spain (onwards: Basque Country) recovers from the COVID-19 crisis. These trends will impact some sectors, places and groups more than others, raising the prospect of greater labour market inequalities (OECD, 2020[1]). To analyse these trends, this chapter is structured in three sections: section 1.1 provides an overview of the initial effects of the COVID-19 lockdown measures on the labour market in the Basque Country; section 1.2 presents OECD estimates of automation on jobs in the region; while section 1.3 looks at recent trends in job quality.

2.1. COVID-19 will have unequal impacts on workers, firms and places

2.1.1. Policy measures helped limit surges in unemployment due to the pandemic

In 2020, the COVID-19 pandemic prompted governments to put in place lockdown measures to slow the spread of the virus, saving lives and reducing strain on health systems. The measures halted economic activity across the globe, precipitating a recession across OECD countries. In 2020, the European Union's (EU) and Spain's real GDP are set to contract by over 8.3% and 10.9% respectively due to the COVID-19 crisis (European Commission, 2020[2]). This unprecedented situation comes at a time when the Basque Country was still recovering from the 2008 and 2010 economic shocks.

Lessons from the past can help inform how the COVID-19 labour shock could impact the Basque region over both the short- and long-term. In 2007, unemployment in the Basque Country reached 7.4%, compared to 8.2% in Spain and 5.8% in the OECD (Figure 2.1). The two waves of the 2008 economic crisis, however, pushed unemployment to a high of 16.7% and 26.3% in the Basque Country and Spain respectively in 2013. During this time, the OECD average was already recovering, reaching 7.9% in 2013. In 2019, the Basque unemployment rate was 2.6% higher than its 2008 level, sitting at 9.3%, showing the local labour market had not yet fully recovered. In 2019, this rate situated the region below the Spanish average of over 14.1%, but above the OECD average of 5.4%.

Between January and June 2020, unemployment rose from 11.0% to 13.5% in the Basque Country, showing the initial effects of lockdown measures and other disruptions (Figure 2.1). Although the lengthy employment shock that followed the 2008 crisis may indicate a prolonged recovery after the pandemic, other factors will also determine the duration and severity of the labour market crisis. For example, the "double-dip" nature of the 2008 crisis in Spain, with its second wave of consequences in 2010, suggests the effects of the COVID-19 crisis may be shorter or longer depending on a second shock. Increases in unemployment may also be set to continue through 2020 and 2021, particularly depending on how redundancy restrictions and other measures are loosened.

The Spanish government put in place a host of measure to help contain the economic consequences of the lockdown measures. In particular, the government implemented a EUR 138.2 billion fiscal package, including EUR 4.3 billion for health measures and EUR 19.2 billion to support employment, notably though *Expedientes de regulación temporal de empleo* (ERTEs), or Short Time Work (STW) schemes that allow workers to obtain unemployment benefits (OECD, 2020[3]). At the regional level, the Basque government has put in place a COVID-19 programme entailing EUR 841 million, including EUR 500 million to support self-employed workers and SMEs (Gobierno Vasco, 2020[4]). Outside of this main package, the Basque government is also supporting the teleworking capacity of Basque SMEs during the pandemic. The region put in place a EUR 2 360 000 fund to co-finance the acquisition of teleworking equipment for Basque companies and the EUR 390 000 INPLANTALARIAK programme to consult SMEs and self-employed workers on teleworking measures (Gobierno Vasco, 2020[4]).

Figure 2.1. Employment-support measures are helping limit surges in unemployment in the Basque Country, though the crisis has reversed years of recovery

Unemployment rate 2007-June 2020, the Basque Country versus Spain and the OECD

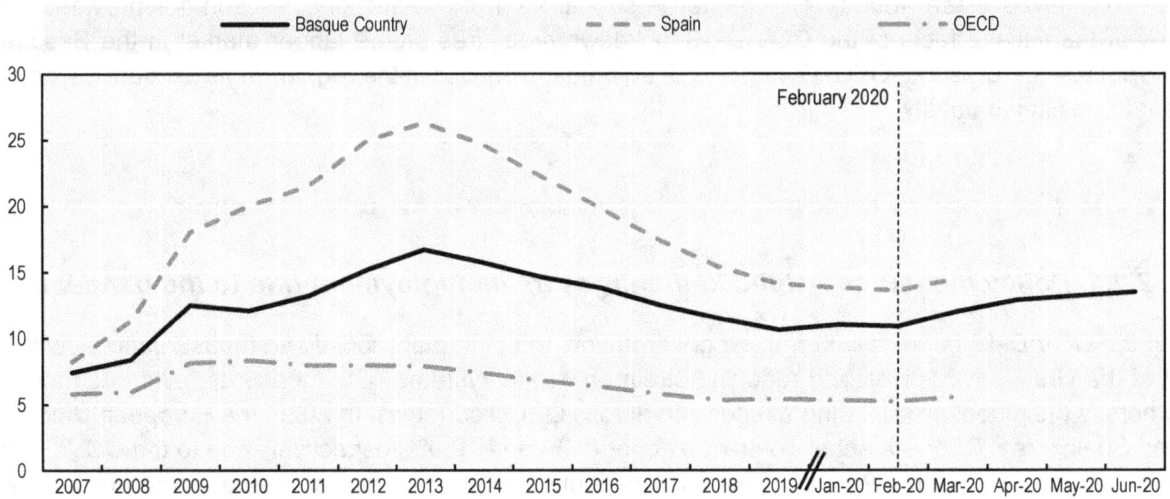

Note: Spain and OECD data reflect latest available data from OECD Statistics, data for the Basque Country from Lanbide. Data is Unemployment Rate (% unemployed over labour force, 15-64 years old).
Source: Lanbide and OECD Statistics.

2.1.2. A relatively high share of jobs can be carried out remotely in the Basque Country, an important factor for regional resilience

Facing a shutdown of all non-essential economic activity in March 2020, Basque enterprises adopted large-scale teleworking measures when possible to continue economic activity. Not all activities, however, can be performed remotely due to the nature of tasks performed, creating inequalities between occupations and sectors. The Basque Country appears as the Spanish region with the third-largest share of jobs that can be performed remotely. In the region, an estimated 32% of total jobs can be carried out remotely, compared to 31% average in Spain. The share of jobs that can be carried out remotely is only larger in Catalonia and the Madrid region, where 33% and 41% of jobs respectively can be done remotely (Figure 2.2).

The relatively high share of jobs amenable to remote work in the Basque Country may be explained by different factors. In particular, the Basque Country's high level of educational attainment may support its teleworking capacity, as a strong statistical correlation has been found between educational attainmant and teleworking capacity (Özgüzel, Veneri and Ahrend, 2020[5]). The Basque Country's teleworking capacity is also supported by its high urban density, as cities typically benefit from more developed internet infrastructure, enabling the region to leverage teleworking capacity (Özgüzel, Veneri and Ahrend, 2020[5]).

In a cross-national comparison, however, the share of jobs amenable to teleworking in the Basque Country is below averages in neighbouring countries. Across the OECD, an average of 34% of jobs can be carried out remotely, 2% above the proportion in the Basque Country. In France, Germany and Portugal the share of jobs that can be carried out remotely reaches national averages of 39%, 36% and 34% respectively, compared to 31% in Spain (Özgüzel, Veneri and Ahrend, 2020[5]).

Large-scale remote work has also revealed differences between sectors and occupations. Across the EU-27, the European Commission's Joint Research Centre (JRC) estimated 40% of IT and communication service workers already worked remotely regularly or with some frequency before COVID-19, while this rate was low in sectors such as manufacturing (JRC, 2020[6]). This divide between higher and lower skill occupations can help guide policy decisions about employment protection and support for teleworking among occupations most vulnerable to lockdown measures.

Figure 2.2. The Basque Country is well positioned for teleworking among Spanish regions

Percent (%) of jobs that can be carried out remotely

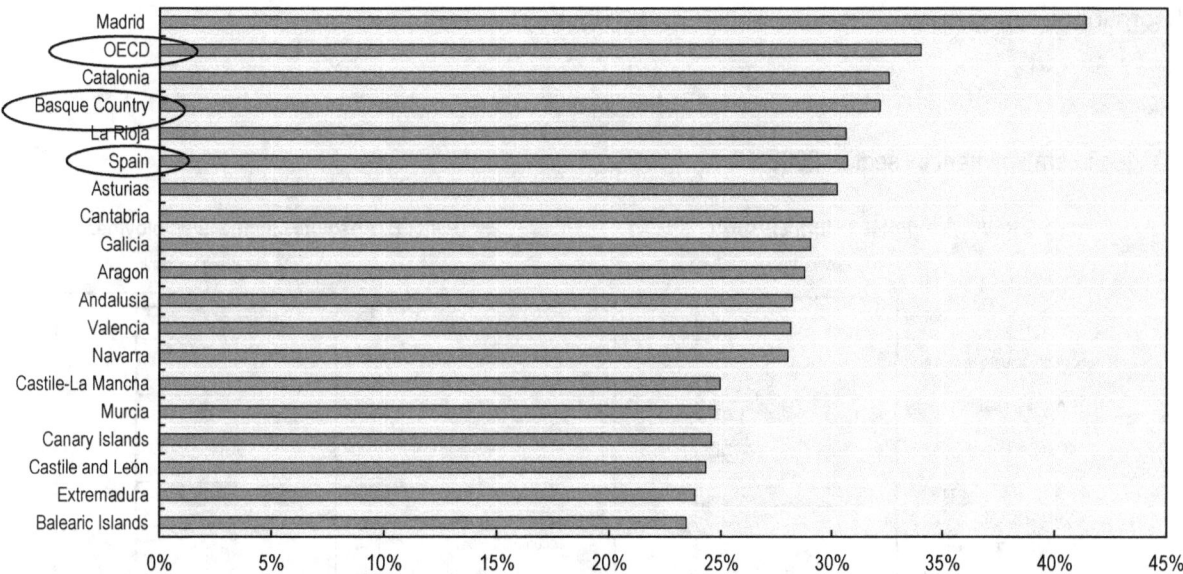

Note: The number of jobs in each country or region that can be carried out remotely as the percentage of total jobs. Regions are ranked in descending order by the share of jobs in total employment that can be done remotely. Ceuta and Melila removed due to size differences.
Source: Source data from EU-LFS survey; calculations from OECD (2020), Capacity for remote working can affect shutdowns' costs differently across places, OECD Policy Note http://www.oecd.org/coronavirus/policy-responses/capacity-for-remote-working-can-affect-lockdown-costs-differently-across-places-0e85740e/

StatLink ᐅ https://doi.org/10.1787/888934188348

2.1.3. Job loss was concentrated in construction and industrial manufacturing between 2008 and 2017

Driven by the collapse of a real estate bubble and a global decline in trade, after 2008 job loss in the Basque labour market were concentrated in construction and industrial manufacturing. Jobs in construction fell from representing nearly 10% of the Basque Country's labour market in 2008 to under 5% in 2017, now lower than both the Spanish and OECD averages (Figure 2.3). The collapse of this sector has had a lasting influence on the composition of unemployed workers, as in 2016, 19.3% of the very long-term unemployed and 9.2% of the long-term unemployed in Spain still came from the construction sector (Bentolila, Jansen and García-Pérez, 2017[7]). The Basque Country also lost nearly 2.5 percentage points of its industrial manufacturing jobs over this period, compared to 3.2 percentage points in Spain. In the region, these losses represented 50 300 construction jobs and 51 300 in industrial manufacturing. Meanwhile, employment in public administration, defence, education, human health and social work activities grew, representing 27 200 jobs, or a growth of 1.4 percentage points.

As employment decreases sharply in manufacturing and non-tradeable sectors over the 2008-2017 period, productivity stayed positive. Between 2008 and 2011, labour productivity in manufacturing increased by 3.4 percentage points while it increased by 3 percentage points in non-tradeable services, including the region's construction sector (Figure 2.3). These increases, however, were likely driven by large job suppression in these sectors, entailing a passive form of productivity growth (Orkestra, 2019[8]). In the manufacturing sector, employment loss and productivity rises showed signs of continuing through the 2008-2017 period, with a 0.8 percentage point loss of employment and an increase of 2.7 percentage points in productivity, indicating the sector was still experiencing the effects of the 2008 and 2011 downturns. In tradeable services, meanwhile, job loss also accompanied productivity decline between 2008 and 2011, as productivity fell by 1.2 percentage points and the sector lost 2 800 jobs. Between 2008 and 2017, a partial recovery in non-tradeable service employment accompanied by productivity growth of 1.4 percentage points may indicate a non-passive form of productivity growth driven by technology absorption, training or skill acquisition (OECD, 2018[9]).

Figure 2.3. The 2008 crisis hit employment hardest in the construction and industrial sectors

Changes in employment by sector, 2008-17

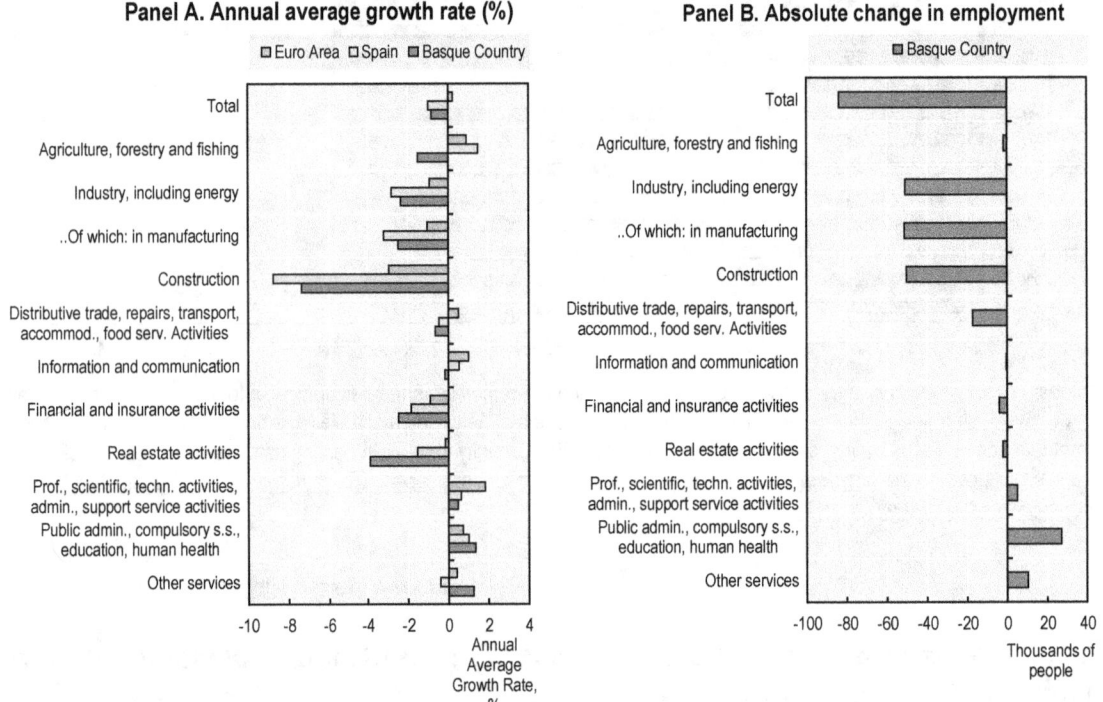

Note: Reference year 2015. Percentage change is calculated as the annual compound growth rate.
Source: OECD Regional database and Annual National Accounts.

Figure 2.4. Productivity increases struggled to accompany employment growth following the 2008 crisis

Employment and labour productivity growth in Basque Country (Spain) by sector

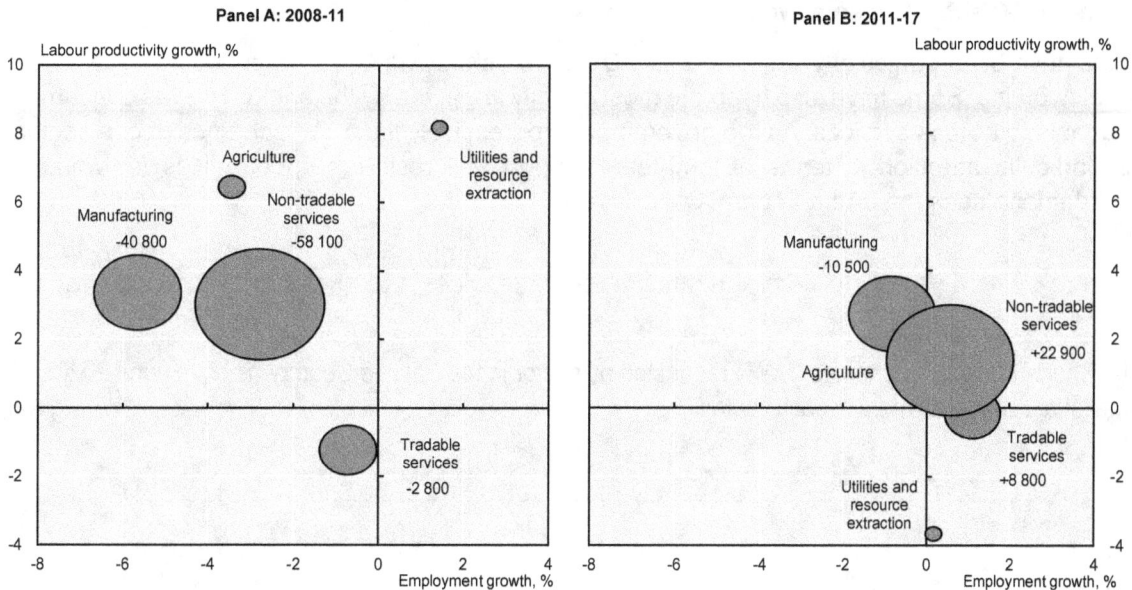

Note: Labour productivity is real gross value added in USD in constant 2015 prices and PPPs per worker. Employment change is the total change in employment over the period, bubble size indicates the size of the sector in terms of employment in 2000. Tradable services are taken as information and communication (J), financial and insurance activities (K), and other services (RSTU). Non-tradable services are composed of construction, distributive trade, repairs, transport, accommodation, food services activities (GHI), real estate activities (L), business services (MN), and public administration (OPQ). Real estate activities are excluded in this chart.
Source: Calculations based on OECD Regional Statistics [Database].

2.1.4. Unlike 2008, employment in retail trade, food service and accommodation is particularly at risk from COVID-19

Initial evidence from the COVID-19 crisis shows that lockdown measures will effect employment disproportionately in the industrial manufacturing, tourism and retail sectors. The Spanish government lifted its initial lockdown measures from 10 May 2020 onwards, though has not lifted large-scale Spanish Short Term Work (STW) schemes. Indeed, *Expedientes de Regulación Temporal de Empleo* (ERTE), Spanish STW schemes, can serve as a gauge of the most distressed sectors.

Employment in food services and accommodation shows one of the highest signs of distress as lockdown measures prevented restaurants, bars and hotels from operating during March-May 2020. This sector, heavily driven by tourism in Spain, accounted for about one-fifth of STW requested in the Basque Country to Spain's government as of 10 June 2020, for a sector that represents around 6.2% of the region's jobs (Figure 2.5). This sector is likely to face a prolonged recovery as an uncertain recovery unfolds, especially in the prospect of new lockdown measures. Indeed, OECD analysis on the initial effects of lockdown measures show large differences in unemployment risk across regions may be partially accounted for by the size of the tourism sector (OECD, 2020[1]).

As in the previous crisis, the Basque Country's large industrial manufacturing sector was also severely impacted. As of 10 June 2020, around one-third of STW requested in the Basque Country came from industrial manufacturing, for a sector representing 20.4% of total employment. As STW and other policy measures are lifted, employment in sectors such as retail and wholesale trade will also be at particular risk of destruction, as trade demand is set for a slow recovery in the face of uncertainty and possible new lockdown measures. According to OECD estimates, up to 10% of employment in the Basque Country involves retail and wholesale trade (Figure 2.6). Other key sectors at risk include art and entertainment, which the OECD estimates accounts for nearly 7% of employment in the region. Construction, on the forefront of the 2008 crisis, meanwhile, accounts for only 3.6% of STW requested as of 10 June 2020, for a sector that represents 6.1% of employment.

These sectors have been particularly vulnerable to COVID-19 as they have not have been able to turn to large-scale teleworking. Some have also been the most directly impacted by the shutdowns, as consumers have been unable to access services. As the government progressively lifts STW schemes, these sectors will require particular attention in terms of long-term support and reskilling opportunities for workers, particularly if demand does not return to pre-COVID levels.

Figure 2.5. Employment in industrial manufacturing, food services and accommodation showed the greatest signs of distress

Share of total Short Time Work Schemes (SWT) requested by sector in the Basque Country as of 10 June 2020 relative to total share of employment in each sector

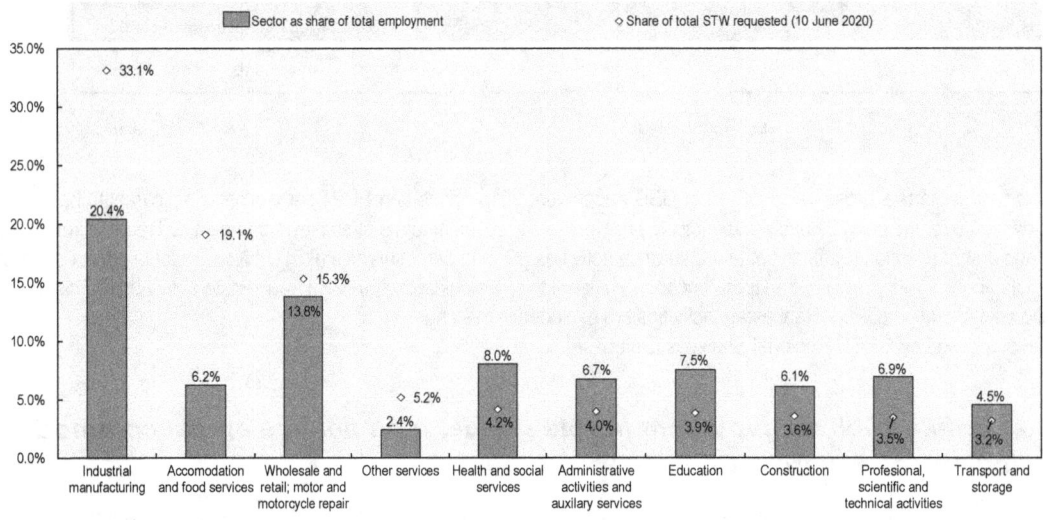

Note 1: ERTE (Expedientes de regulación temporal de empleo) are STW schemes in Spain. ERTE requested are STW requested by the Basque government to the central Spanish administration. Only top ten sector requesting ERTE are listed in the figure.
Note 2: Shares of total employment reflect 2019.
Source: Dirección de Trabajo, Gobierno Vasco; Futurelan, Lanbide Servicio Vasco de Empleo.

Figure 2.6. OECD calculations show trade-related employment at particularly high risk in the Basque Country

Risk from Covid by sector, TL2, 2017

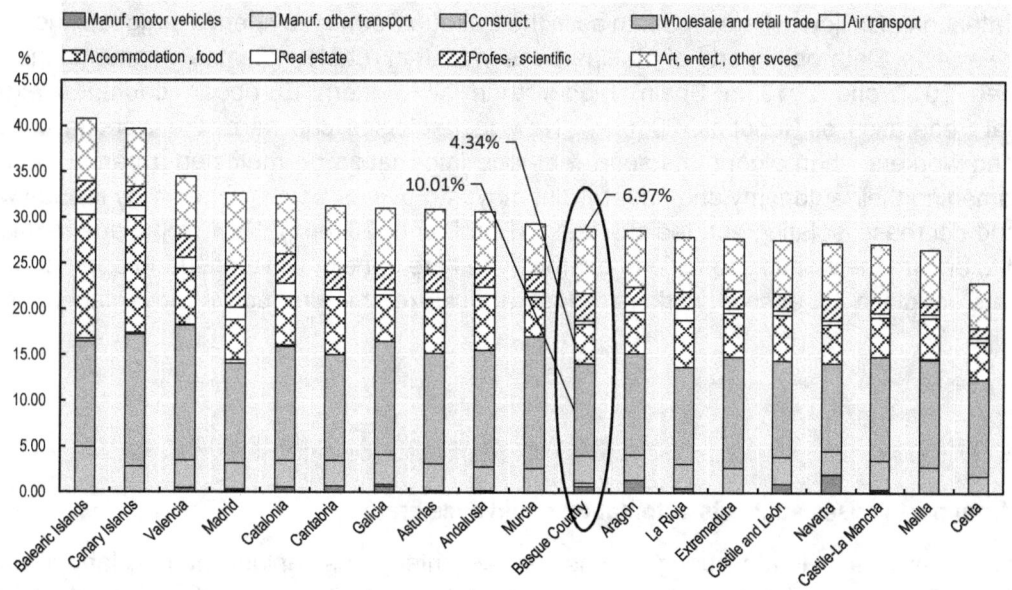

Note: Share of employment in sector at risk.
Source: Eurostat - Regional Structural Business Statistics (table sbs_r_nuts06_r2)

StatLink https://doi.org/10.1787/888934188367

2.2. What will be the impacts of automation in the Basque Country?

2.2.1. *A higher share of jobs are at high risk of automation in the Basque Country than the OECD average*

Automation has the potential to raise competitiveness and improve working conditions, though it can also supress jobs. The OECD considers a job at **significant** risk of change if 50% to 70% of the tasks within the job are vulnerable to automation, while those at **high** risk have more than 70% of tasks that could be replaced by a machine (Nedelkoska and Quintini, 2018[10]). When considering both jobs at high and significant risk, a smaller proportion of the overall labour market is vulnerable to automation in the Basque Country than all other Spanish regions, outside of Madrid, Ceuta and Melilla (Figure 2.7). Indeed, in Spain, 55% of jobs are at overall risk of automation compared to 54% in the Basque Country.

The Basque Country, however, has a significantly higher portion of jobs at high risk of automation compared to the OECD average. In the Basque Country, 22.2% are at high risk of automation compared to 14% across OECD countries, putting over 205 000 jobs in the region at high risk of suppression (Figure 2.7). Concerning high risk jobs, only Slovakia, Slovenia and Greece have a larger share of jobs at high risk of automation than Spain. The importance of industrial manufacturing as an employer in the Basque Country could be driving the region's vulnerability to job automation. The sector tends to include a large share of jobs involving routine and non-cognitive tasks, at higher risk of replacement by technology. Moreover, evidence from past recessions indicate the region's vulnerability to automation may increase with the COVID-19 crisis, as firms turn to automation to restructure production and cut costs (Box 2.1).

The region, meanwhile, has a nearly equal share of jobs at risk of significant change due to automation as the OECD average, with 293 000 jobs at risk, or 31.8% of total jobs, compared to 31.6% across the OECD.

For those at high risk, this entails a risk of job suppression, while those at significant risk face change in the way these jobs are performed as many tasks becomes automated, calling for new skills to remain in the job (Nedelkoska and Quintini, 2018[10]) (see Box 2.2 for more information on the OECD methodology).

Indeed, the digitalisation of the workplace involves changes to the workplace beyond suppression that require the attention of policymakers. In Spain as in the Basque Country, evidence suggests these changes may be accelerating. Data on imports of multipurpose industrial robots indicates shipments increased by 12% between 2017 and 2018 in Spain, higher than all western European countries except Italy (International Federation of Robotics, 2018[11]). New technologies can harm the working conditions of manufacturing workers when algorithms send real-time information on their performance to centralised systems, damaging their autonomy and privacy, but may improve job quality when they reduce workplace accidents and decrease isolating and tedious tasks (Eurofound, 2018[12]). New workplace regulations will be required to ensure the working conditions of employees are upheld, while ensuring appropriate training measures are in place to ensure workers adapt and seize the productive advantages brought by technology.

> **Box 2.1. COVID-19 is likely to accelerate the uptake of labour-saving technologies**
>
> **Evidence from pasts crises suggests automation could accelerate**
>
> Automation tends to accelerate during recessions, as enterprises replace human labour with cost-saving robots. Research, such as that by Hershbein and Kahn (2018), indicates routine job loss may explain the phenomenon of "jobless" recoveries in the United States, during which employment does not recover in certain sectors. According to this research, companies in the most heavily affected areas by the 2008 crisis in the United States tended to supress jobs in routine occupations, while hiring a greater share of higher skilled workers and increasing investments in capital. In particular, routine occupations involving manual tasks are found to have suffered the sharpest decline in employment share. The authors found that the hardest-hit US metropolitan areas were 5% more likely to contain education and experience requirements in job postings after the 2009 crisis, and 2-3% more likely to include cognitive or computer skill requirements. At the same time, firms increased investments in computers.
>
> This risk of automation is compounded in the face of COVID-19, as routine occupations are particularly common in some of the hardest hit sectors such as industrial manufacturing, transportation and food services. In lead firms, particularly those who faced large supply chain disruptions due to COVID-19, companies may also automate production hand-in-hand with a reshoring global value chains as industry 4.0 technologies allow for more rapid adjustments to fluctuating demand.
>
> Source: (Hershbein and Kahn, 2018[13]) (Muro, Maxim and Whiton, 2020[14])

Automation is also likely to generate inequalities between population groups within the Basque Country, as different groups tend to occupy jobs at higher or lower risk of automation. In the region, 51% of men and 57% of immigrants occupy jobs at risk of automation, making them particularly vulnerable (Figure 2.8). Men and immigrants tend to be overrepresented in the construction and the manufacturing sectors, where AI and other technologies may restructure production processes. 48% of women, meanwhile, occupy jobs at some risk of automation. Women may be at less risk as this groups tends to occupy less routine service jobs, in which less tasks that may be replaced by technology.

Multiple factors influence and structure job supression and change, determining the actual displacement of automatable jobs. Indeed, the effects of automation are determined by the rate at which technology is introduced, the way workers adapt as well as multiple differences in work organisation across countries and regions (Orkestra, 2019[15]). The social acceptability or the economic profitability of automation, also help weigh into the actual supression of a task or job at risk of automation (Le Ru, 2016[16]). Demand-side policies also play a role in the way automation unfolds. In the Basque Country, industrial and innovation strategies such as Basque Industry 4.0 and the region's Smart Specialisation Strategy (RIS3) are encouraging this process of automation within firms, calling for attention on its effects on the workplace.

Figure 2.7. More jobs in the Basque Country are high risk compared to the OECD average, though less than all other regions in Spain

Risk of automation by region in Spain, 2018

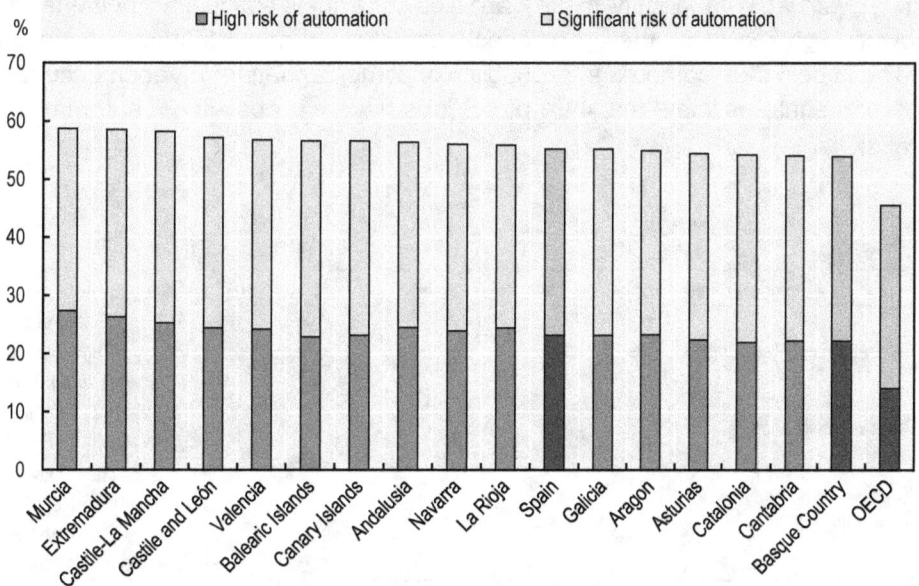

Note: Data for Spain and Spanish regions is 2018 . Due to the small number of observations, Ceuta and Melilla are from the figure. Also Madrid is excluded from the figure.
Source: OECD calculations based on the European Labour Force Survey for Spain and Spanish regions. OECD calculations are based on the Survey of Adult Skills (PIAAC) (2012); and Nedelkoska, L. and G. Quintini (2018), "Automation, skills use and training", OECD Social, Employment and Migration Working Papers, No. 202, https://doi.org/10.1787/2e2f4eea-en.

StatLink https://doi.org/10.1787/888934188386

Box 2.2. How does the OECD calculate the risk of job automation?

The Programme for the International Assessment of Adult Competencies (PIACC)

Frey and Osborne (FO) estimated the number of occupations at high risk of automation in the United States using a two-step methodology. They conducted a workshop with a group of experts in machine learning, whom they provided with a list of 70 occupations and their corresponding O*NET task descriptions. Experts were asked "Can the tasks of this job be sufficiently specified, conditional on the availability of big data, to be performed by state of the art computer-controlled equipment?". This allowed for the coding of each occupation as automatable or non-automatable. FO then used a machine learning algorithm to find out more about the links between the coding to automate and the list of O*NET variables. They were able to identify those variables (and their associated bottlenecks) with higher prediction power. High scores on these bottlenecks are likely to mean that an occupation is safe from automation. They could then compute a "probability of computerisation" for each occupation in the US, leading to the aggregate estimate that 47% of US jobs have a probability of automation of more than 70%.

Table 2.1. Automation bottlenecks

Computerisation bottleneck	O*NET variable
Perception and Manipulation	Finger dexterity
	Manual dexterity
	Cramped workspace; awkward positions
Creative intelligence	Originality
	Fine arts
Social intelligence	Social perceptiveness
	Negotiation
	Persuasion
	Assisting and caring for others

Note: Please refer to (Frey and Osborne, 2013[17]) for further details on the definition of automation bottlenecks.
Source: (Frey and Osborne, 2013[17])

Building on this approach, (Nedelkoska and Quintini, 2018[10])(NQ) calculated the risk of automation across 32 OECD countries. The approach is based on individual-level data from the OECD Survey of Adult Skills (PIAAC), providing information on the skills composition of each person's job and their skillset. While drawing on FO, this methodology presents four main differences: (i) training data in the NQ model is taken from Canada to exploit the country's large sample in PIAAC; (ii) O*NET occupational data for FO's 70 original occupations were manually recoded into the International Standard Classification of Occupations (ISCO); (iii) NQ uses a logistic regression compared to FO's Gaussian process classifier; (iv) NQ found equivalents in PIAAC to match FO's bottlenecks. While PIAAC includes variables addressing the bottlenecks identified by FO, no perfect match exists for each variable. No question in PIAAC could be identified to account for job elements related to "assisting and caring for others", related to occupations in health and social services. This implies that risks of automation based on NQ could be slightly overestimated.

Note: Please refer to (Nedelkoska and Quintini, 2018[10]) for further details on the definition of the PIAAC variables.
Source: (Nedelkoska and Quintini, 2018[10]). (OECD, 2018[18]).

Figure 2.8. Men and immigrants tend to occupy jobs with tasks more likely to be automated

Average risk of automation by population group, 2018

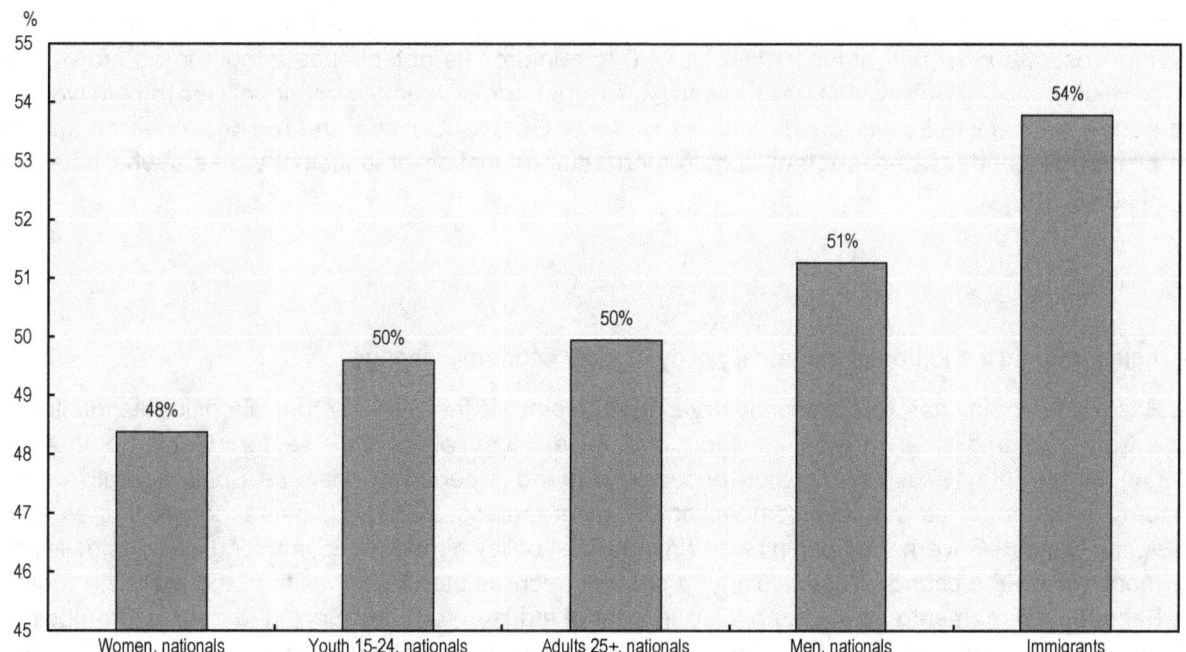

Source: OECD calculations on Labour Force Survey.

2.2.2. Automation may accentuate longer term trends, putting industrial employment at risk in the region

The three occupations at high risk of automation with the greatest number of workers are all closely associated with the Basque industrial manufacturing sector (Table 2.2). These include:

- *Stationary plant and machine operators* constitute the largest pool of workers at high risk of automation, representing over 23 000 workers in the region;
- *Metal, machinery and related trades workers* represent the second-largest occupation group at high risk from automation in terms of number of workers, with 19 700 jobs at high risk.
- *Drivers and mobile plant operators* represent the third-largest group, constituting 17 500 jobs at high risk of automation.

Automation of key industrial occupations may accelerate the relative and absolute decrease in industrial employment already underway in the region. This should be of particular concern in the Basque Country, as the region's industrial base has been at the heart of its growth model since the 1980s, when the region leaned on industrial policies to redevelop its manufacturing sector (Box 2.3). Since 2000, industry, including the energy sector, has decreased from nearly 28% of total employment to 20% in 2017, compared to a smaller decrease in Spain, from 18% in 2000 to 12.3% in 2017 (Figure 2.9). During the 2008 economic crisis and its aftermath, between 2008 and 2015, the Basque Country lost 64 000 jobs in the sector, representing nearly 25% of sectoral employment.

The Basque Government has put industrial development at the heart of its new industrial strategy, seeing the sector a means to reduce unemployment, consolidate recovery, and raise social cohesion (Gobierno Vasco, 2017[19]). To do so, the region has put in place an Industry 4.0 policy, a process in which "the physical world of industrial production merges with the digital world of information technology – in other words, the creation of a digitized and interconnected industrial production, also known as cyber-physical systems" (UNIDO, 2017[20]). This involves supporting struggling firms and reinforcing financing instruments, particularly related to digitalisation, for example by promoting new industrial-technological projects and supporting digitalisation. The region, however, recognises the loss of lower-skilled industrial jobs as a major risk of the fourth industrial revolution in the Basque Country's Employment Strategy 2020 (Gobierno Vasco, 2016[21]). In order for Industry 4.0 to reinforce its potential as a tool for job growth and social cohesion, regional innovation policies can work in tandem with employment policies to help workers prepare for a 4.0 setting. For instance, in the province of Ontario, Canada, the regional government has put in place a Second Career Program to help fund adult education of industrial workers who have lost their jobs (Box 2.4).

> ### Box 2.3. Basque industrial reconversion in 1980-1990
>
> **The region inherits a tradition of industrial policy to steer economic change**
>
> The Basque economy has relied on industry since the start of the 20th century. Traditional industries range from iron and steel to machine tools and an auxiliary automotive sector (Gobierno Vasco, 2009[22]). In the late 1970s, the Basque economy entered a period of crisis as Spain liberalised its economy, toughening international competition (Gobierno Vasco, 2009[22]). As a response, in the early 1980s, the Basque Government put in place an industrial policy aimed at reconverting, reindustrialising and modernising the economy, particularly in sectors such as steel, shipbuilding and machine tools. The Basque Departamento de Industria (Department of Industry) and the Sociedad para la Promoción y Reconversión Industrial (SPRI) led this policy regionally, complementing the national Plan de Reconversión Industrial Sectorial (1980-1986). The Industry Department tended to lead more traditional industrial policies, associated with investments and restructuring, while the SPRI directed innovation programmes. Such innovation policies were varied, ranging from specific programmes for greater inclusion of technologies in companies, to efforts to internationalise Basque companies.
>
> As part of this strategy, the Basque Country stimulated industry-business "clusters". Ahedo (2004) defines clusters as: "a specific kind of sector or specialized field involving competing and cooperating firm concentrations, with a dense presence of small and medium-sized enterprises (SMEs), in a proximate relational environment and with a supporting role of some public and semi-public or civic institutions." Within clusters, two types of relationships exist, those among firms and those between firms and institutions, such as chambers of commerce or public institutions. When first launched in the early 1990s, "cluster" policy entailed the creation of new tripartite institutions, such as an economic and social council, as well as industry-level working groups, tasked with assembling joint competitiveness programmes. Cluster development is marked by the region's tradition of cooperation, worker-participation and incremental technology assimilation. The tradition of cluster-development continues to today, with the activity of partnerships and dialogue among firms and between firms and regional institutions. According to Ahedo (2004), cluster development has helped create a stronger system of industrial associations and collaboration between industry and the region's government.
>
> Source: Ahedo, M. (2004), "Cluster policy in the Basque country (1991–2002): constructing 'industry–government' collaboration through cluster-associations", *European Planning Studies*, Vol. 12/8, pp. 1097-1113; Del Castillo, J. and J. Paton (2010), "Política de promoción y reconversión industrial", *EKONOMIAZ. Revista vasca de Economía*, Vol. 25/3, pp. 96-123, http://www.euskadi.eus/web01-a2reveko/es/k86aEkonomiazWar/ekonomiaz/abrirArticulo?idpubl=70&registro=1063.

Table 2.2. Industrial jobs in the Basque Country are at particular risk of destruction or change due to automation

Top 10 occupations with greater number of people with jobs at high risk of automation in the Basque Country, 2018

Occupation	Number of people at high risk, thousands	High risk, %	Number of people at significant risk, thousands	Risk of significant change, %	Total people at risk
Stationary Plant and Machine Operators	23 200	48	15 400	32	38 60
Metal, Machinery and Related Trades Workers	19 700	31	18 200	28	37 90
Drivers and Mobile Plant Operators	17 500	45	15 200	39	32 70
Cleaners and Helpers	15 100	32	26 900	56	42 00
Personal Care Workers	14 000	39	11 400	32	25 40
Sales Workers	11 700	17	24 300	34	36 00
Personal Services Workers	11 500	25	17 000	37	28 50
Numerical and Material Recording Clerks	10 400	31	9 700	29	20 10
Assemblers	8 400	44	10 500	56	18 90
Building and Related Trades Workers (excluding Electricians)	7 900	30	8 800	34	16 700

Note: The 100% estimate for Assemblers is due to statistical uncertainty. High rates of automation for this occupation correspond to prior OECD research.
Source: OECD calculations based on the European Labour Force Survey.

Figure 2.9. Automation may accelerate losses in industrial employment

Employment in industry, including energy as a proportion of total employment, 2000-18, Basque Country versus Spain and the OECD average

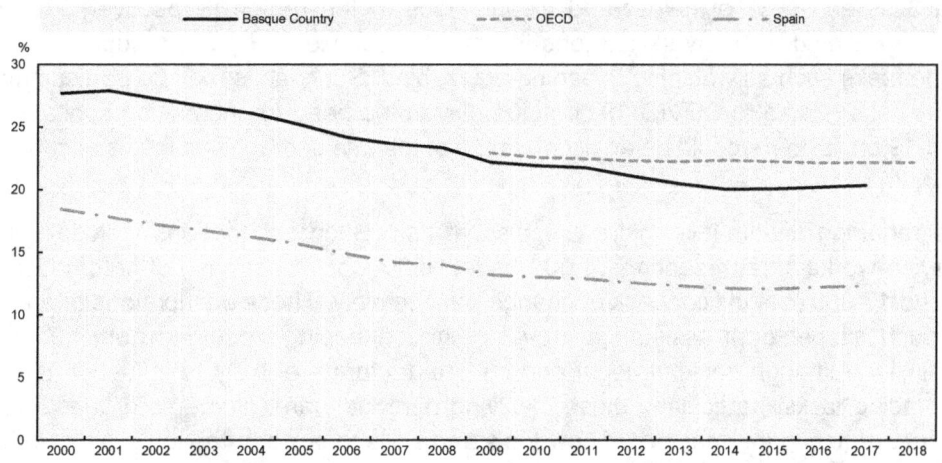

Note: Data is Regional Employment at place of work, total activities and employment in industry including energy for Spain and Basque Country. Data for OECD is industry including construction employment in thousands as a share of employment in thousands.
Source: OECD Regional Database and OECD Employment in thousands and OECD employment by industry.

> **Box 2.4. International good practice: Supporting mid-career workers in the industrial sector in Ontario, Canada**
>
> **The Second Career Programme**
>
> The Province of Ontario, Canada has a labour force of 12.1 million people (15 years and older) with an unemployment rate of 5.7% before COVID-19. As of 2019, there were about 761 000 people working within the province's manufacturing sector. The sector as a whole went through significant structural change over the last ten years. To help workers within the sector change jobs that were at risk of downsizing, the Ontario government introduced the Second Career programme. Second Career is for laid-off unemployed workers for which skills training is the most appropriate intervention to transition them into high-skill, in- demand occupations in the local labour market. Workers can receive up to up to CAD 28,000 for costs including: tuition, books, manuals, workbooks or other instructional costs, transportation, basic living allowance (maximum CAD 410 per week), and child care. The programme represents an intensive government investment in retraining workers for in-demand jobs, enabling them to go back to school for up to two years to retrain for a new job.
>
> Individuals can apply to the programme if they receive employment insurance. Applications require candidates to describe how long they have been unemployed or holding a temporary job, positions they have applied for, level of education, prior positions, skills possessed and skills sought and information that shows how the skills and job are in-demand. The programme also asks candidates to submit personal financial information and submit details of relevant training institutions.
>
> Source: OECD (2014), *Employment and Skills Strategies in Canada*, OECD Reviews on Local Job Creation, OECD Publishing, Paris, https://dx.doi.org/10.1787/9789264209374-en.; Ontario Ministry of Labour, Training and Skills Development (2020), *Second Career*, Toronto, Canada https://www.ontario.ca/page/second-career

2.2.3. Service jobs are also at risk of automation, particularly in sectors vulnerable to COVID-19

Although less concentrated by sector, multiple service-related occupations in the Basque Country face automation risks. Cleaners and helpers constitute the largest category of people at high risk of seeing their occupation disappear or change significantly, with 15 100 people at high risk and 26 900 at significant risk, representing 32% and 56% of helper and cleaner jobs in the region respectively (Table 2.3). These positions are associated with low skilled jobs in both the service and good-producing sectors, that can involve routine tasks such as watching, cleaning or washing. Such tasks may be particularly vulnerable to automation as risks related to COVID-19 continue. Given the need for increasing sanitary measures due to the COVID-19 crisis, there could be an acceleration of the use of machines in this occupational category to mitigate health risks.

Occupations requiring middle-level skills are also at risk. Such occupations include personal care or personal service workers, representing 14 000 and 11 500 jobs at high risk of automation in the region, and 11 400 and 17 000 at significant risk of change, respectively. These occupations often require care for individuals, such as personal assistance, travel or housekeeping, requiring both human contact and middle-level skills. Although societal, legal and cultural factors are likely to influence the automation of such human-facing tasks, particularly those involving personal care, elements of these occupations are likely to change, requiring the mastery of new tools and skills to perform the job. Sales workers, customer service clerks and food preparation assistants also constitute large groups of workers facing high risks of automation in the region, with 11 700, 7 500 and 4 100 jobs at high risk and 24 300, 22 200 and 1 200 at significant risk. Jobs such as clerks are also particularly at risk as secretarial tasks, word processing and other routine data manipulation often constitute a large part of their duties, tasks that are highly susceptible to digitalisation. Although these jobs cover a wide range of service sectors, they are particularly concentrated in sectors showing early and persistent signs of distress due to COVID-19, such as retail trade, accommodation and food services.

Table 2.3 Automatable service-associated jobs are common in sectors at risk from COVID-19

Top 8 occupations associated with services with the greatest number of people with jobs at high risk of automation in the Basque Country, 2018

Occupation	Number of people at high risk, thousands	High risk, %	Number of people at significant risk, thousands	Risk of significant change, %	Total people at risk
Cleaners and Helpers	15 100	32	26 900	56	42 000
Personal Care Workers	14 000	39	11 400	32	25 000
Sales Workers	11 700	17	24 300	34	36 000
Personal Service Workers	11 500	25	17 000	37	28 500
Numerical and Material Recording Clerks	10 400	31	9 700	29	20 100
Customer Service Clerks	7 500	16	22 200	46	29 700
Food Preparation Assistants	4 100	68	1 200	20	5 300
Health Associate Professionals	4 000	31	3 700	29	7 700

Source: OECD calculations based on the European Labour Force Survey.

2.2.4. The Basque Country is gaining industrial jobs, while it loses high-skilled service occupations at lower risk of automation

Three main trends can be identified concerning job creation and automation in the Basque Country between 2008 and 2018.

- (1) First, the Basque Country has been creating jobs in a number of middle skill occupations which are at risk of automation, particularly occupations related to industrial manufacturing.

Job creation in the Basque Country's industrial base is a welcome sign of recovery from the 2008 crisis, and may indicate the region's recent industrial policies have helped restore industrial employment and slow long term trends concerning this sector. However, increases in jobs in these occupations may constitute a risk for these workers as they are among the highest risk occupations, all the more as the region's industrial policies support the sector's digitalisation. For instance, the region created over 12 280 stationary plant and machine operator positions and over 19 000 metal, machinery and related trades workers since 2008 (Figure 2.10).

The region has also created low skill service jobs, including over 13 000 customer service clerks, which are also at high risk of automation. The creation of low skill service jobs has been a pattern seen across Spanish regions, characteristic of Spain's recovery from the 2008 crisis. These occupations are also at particularly risk due to the COVID-19, as sectors such as tourism, accommodation and food services may shed jobs as these sectors undergo a prolonged recovery.

- (2) Second, the region lost employment in certain low and middle-skill occupations at high risk of automation, such as low-skill services.

The region lost 20 298 cleaners and helper positions and 23 845 building and related trades workers (excluding Electricians). These jobs also include occupations linked to industrial manufacturing at high risk of automation, such as drivers and mobile plant operators, an occupation which lost over 7 500 jobs. These changes can reflect structural, technological and policy changes in the Basque Country and Spain since the 2008 and 2010 crises, such as the sharp downturn in the construction sector. As many of the region's unemployed workers may hold the skills from these occupations, this evidence could serve as a basis to tailor adult learning policies and can constitute an opportunity to upskill these parts of the Basque workforce.

- (3) Third, the Basque Country has tended to lose high-skilled jobs at lower risk of automation, with the exception of jobs in education and health.

Principally, this concerns occupations such as business and administration associate professionals, business and administration professionals and legal, social and cultural professional lost employment. The region's RIS3 specialisation strategy, with a volley of policies dedicated to energy and bio-health, may help reverse some of these trends, as growth in these areas may foster increases in high skill occupations at lower risk of automation.

Examples from regions across the OECD could help deepen strategic planning around skills development and demand-side policies to diversify the region's economic base in ways that are complementary to its industrial core. For example, officials in the city of Southampton, United Kingdom, drafted an action plan on the future of work which involved mapping applicable international practices and meeting with city business leaders (Box 2.5). In the same way, in Washington-state United States, a task force made up of elected officials, labour and firms formulated policy recommendations related to the future of work. These involved a wide range of consultations among different stakeholders, ranging from online surveys and meetings to events and in-person consultations with different local actors.

Figure 2.10. The Basque Country has shed high skill occupations at lower risk of automation

Job creation and automation risk by occupation (blue is high-skilled, yellow is middle-skilled, green is low-skilled), 2008-2018

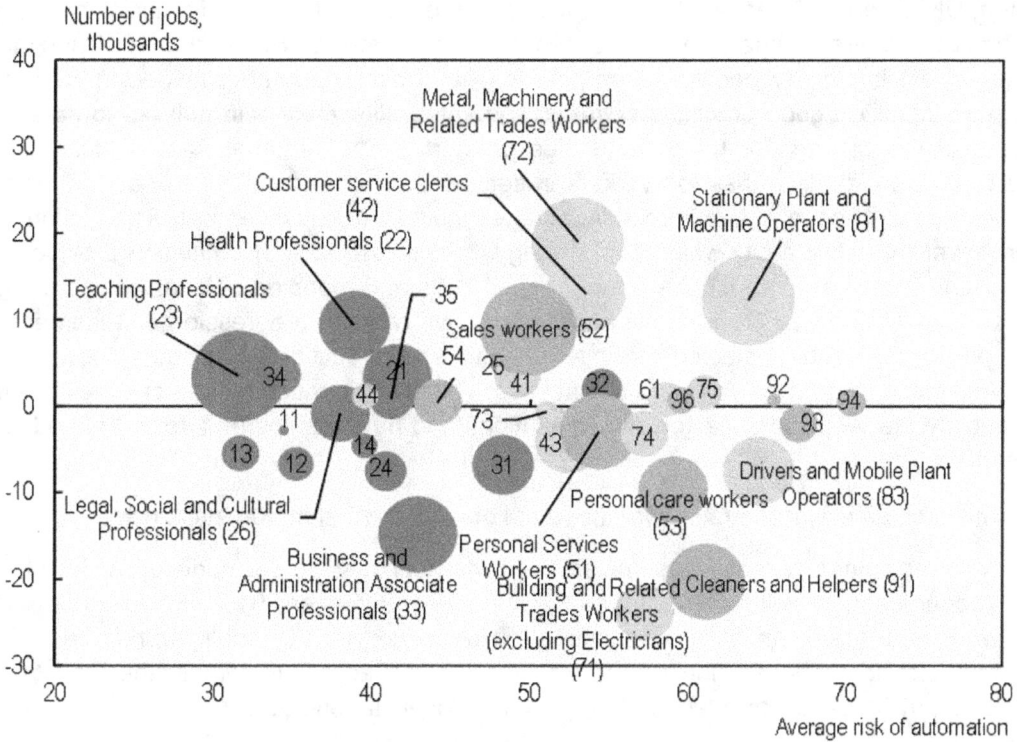

Note: The change in number of jobs in thousands is calculated between 2011-2018. Occupations (ISCO-08 code indicated in the bubble) are ranked from low to high risk of automation along the horizontal axis. Changes in the number of jobs for each occupation are reported along the vertical axis. Bubble size represents the share of jobs in the occupation with respect to total employment in the region.
Source: Calculations based on EU Labour Force survey.

StatLink ⟶ https://doi.org/10.1787/888934188405

> **Box 2.5. Finding synergies between local skills and specialisation strategies**
>
> **Elected officials in Southampton, UK seek international examples and meet with business leaders**
>
> In Southampton, UK, a panel of elected officials inquired on the potential impact of artificial intelligence (AI), robotics and other digital technologies on the local economy. Between September 2018 and March 2019, the group of officials developed an action plan for the city on the future of work. In the inquiry process, the team identified good practices being implemented elsewhere and policies to potentially introduce in the city, including on the opportunities created by AI, automation and technological changes. The team also identified risk for workers in sectors that are most likely to see the greatest increase in the level of use of AI, automation and technological advancement. The action plan envisages the development of a city-wide skills strategy, a skills analysis of education providers, an update of education curricular to enrich the offer of digital skills and mapping of local lifelong learning platforms, particularly to find ways to improve access, improve rates of progression and increase job outcomes. As part of this inquiry, elected officials met with local practitioners in other cities, while a separate team developed a study of the city's businesses. This team identified resources the city could mobilise to stimulate the technology sector, and institutions and partnerships that could help advance the city's objectives.
>
> **Workers and firms articulate a local strategy for the future of work in Washington state, US**
>
> The US state of Washington recently assembled a 16-member task force made up of legislators, business, and labour leaders, which carried out a study between October 2018 and November 2019. The regional workforce board, an office connecting job seekers with the public workforce system, provided staff for the project. The task force performed a number of actions to compile their list of policy recommendations, paying particular attention to the input of local stakeholders:
>
> - Use of online surveys to understand the interests of representatives before a series of meetings;
> - Consultations with local stakeholders, such as municipal governments, labour unions or chambers of commerce;
> - Organisation of events related to the future of work;
> - Compilation of relevant research related to the future of work, particularly concerning the effects of technology on jobs;
>
> Worker representatives highlighted low job quality as a challenge in the region, particularly those posed by digital monitoring tools, while businesses noted staffing difficulties and challenges to best train workers to use advanced technologies. The force formulated joint policy recommendations which included worker upskilling and access to lifelong learning, technology in the workplace, improved labour market data and credentialing transparency, modernisation of worker support systems and equal access to economic development resources across the region.
>
> Source: OECD (2020 forthcoming), OECD Reviews on Local job Creation: Preparing Ontario, Canada for the Future of Work; Washington Workforce training and education coordinating board (2019), Future of work task force 2019 policy report, https://www.wtb.wa.gov/wp-content/uploads/2019/12/Future-of-Work-2019-Final-Report.pdf.

2.2.5. As employment starts to recover, the Basque Country can mobilise new tools to track sectoral change in the region

The Basque public employment service (PES), Lanbide, launched Futurelan, an innovative tool to track the evolution of occupations in the face of the future of work. Futurelan uses past labour market trends to make predictions about the future. This tool provides real and predicted data on evolution, the distribution of employment occupation and the evolution of contracts. Information can be selected according to occupation or sector. Although the COVID-19 crisis is likely to modify conjectures, Futurelan predictions set prior to the crisis foresee nearly 57 000 new jobs in food service, health and safety/security sectors, as well as over 41 000 jobs as accountants, administrative staff and other office employment (Figure 2.11). Meanwhile, the tool predicts a decrease of nearly 19 000 in machine and facility operators and assemblers. Other occupations, such as qualified workers in agriculture, livestock, forestry and fishing and technical and professional staff are also predicted to decrease over time, shedding nearly 7 000 and 5 500 jobs respectively between 2018 and 2030. Futurelan predictions correspond with OECD calculations which suggests a high likelihood of job suppression in machine and facility operators and assemblers.

The tool's prediction model, however, may need to adapt to integrate predictions related to COVID-19. Indeed, Futurelan's prediction of job growth in food services and sales occupations may change significantly as early estimates on the impact of COVID-19 show a significant, and likely prolonged, downturn in the sector. The region could also take this tool further to provide more data on skills trends, beyond sectors and occupations. In this way, tools such as Futurelan could help the region develop policies on how those holding those jobs can retrain for other jobs, putting in place appropriate training to assist job transition. For instance, in Wallonia, Belgium, the region has put in place a sectoral skill analysis that involves carrying out field and expert interviews to identify skills that could arise from emerging sectors (Box 2.6). Reinforcing Futurelan's quantitative predictions with a wider qualitative approach would complement the tool's predictions, receiving direct information from companies and key actors on how they see their sector evolving.

Figure 2.11. Futurelan is a helpful tool to evaluate occupational change of the future in the Basque Country

Projection of net variation of jobs per occupation in the Basque Country, 2018-30

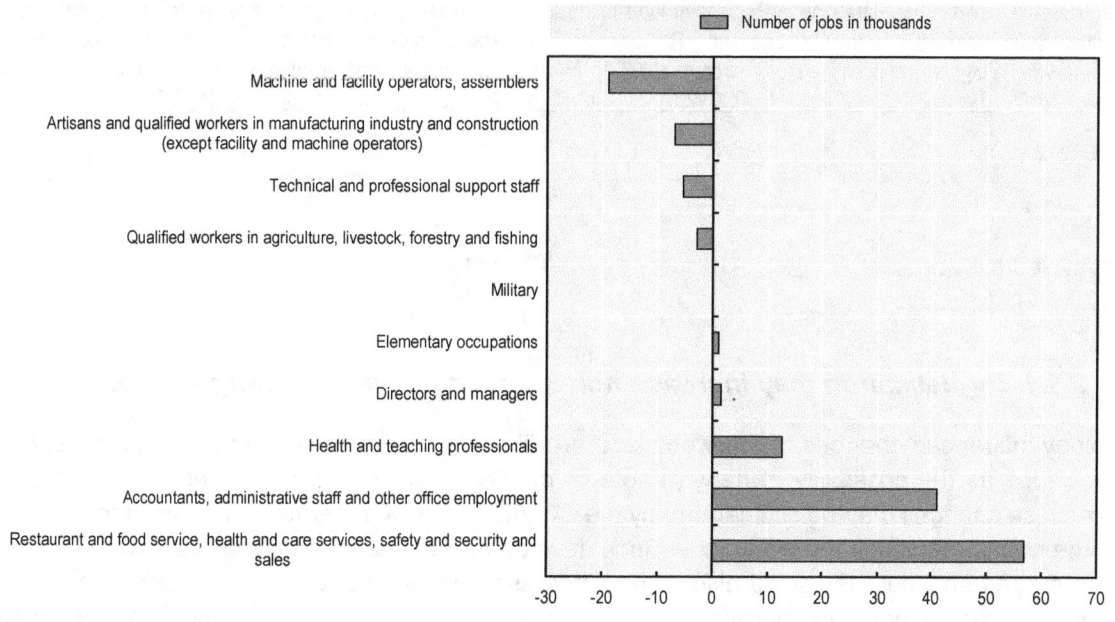

Source: *Lanbide. FutureLan* Observatorio de perspectiva de empleo.

> **Box 2.6. International good practice: Industry skills mapping in Wallonia (Belgium)**
>
> Wallonia's Public Employment Service (PES), Le Forem, undertakes yearly prospective analyses to identify local skills needs in specific sectors. In its Le Forem Study, the PES aimed to develop appropriate training offerings for Wallonia's competitive and business clusters. The analysis first classifies future occupations and associated core skills in eight sectors. It then identifies a set of related or secondary skills that could subsequently arise from developing the sector. The approach follows a five-step qualitative process: (1) Analytical staff from the PES produce occupational reports by sector and (2) disseminate report to sectoral expert groups, composed of internal staff and industry specialists. Then, (3) a method called Abilitic2Perform is used to identify the skills required for each occupation or skills group. Wallonia adopted Abilitic2Perform methods from Interreg IV EU projects in Belgium. Four expert workshops, organised by occupation, identify key evolution factors and the potential evolution scenarios in a six step sub-process. At the end of the Abilitic2Perform process, (4) expert groups select the most likely (or desired) scenario, identifying associated skills needs. Finally, in a final step, (5) the local training department receives the results of the analysis in order to start designing appropriate training programmes, publishing them and forwarding them to relevant training authorities. A panel of experts answers a set of questions that are then included in the sector reports. The objective is to check the sectoral trends and particularly to detect the effects that these trends may have on occupations.
>
> Sectors and associated industries value the programme since they do not have the capacity or resources to undertake such an extensive study, while job seekers and public administrators can benefit from a rich knowledge base about the labour market. Le Forem has built on this methodology to produce an array of yearly analyses that combine data work with qualitative evidence from expert groups, yielding knowledge not only on occupational change but also skills needs. For example, in 2020, Le Forem published Métiers en tension de recrutement en Wallonie which identifies in-demand occupations and the causes for hiring shortages, such as a skills mismatch or poor working conditions. The analysis leans on a three-part methodology, first through a statistical analysis of job offers received by the PES, followed by consultation with expert groups. In a final step, oriented towards implementation, Le Forem communicates the findings to Wallonia's sectoral training funds, a body run by social partners that helps define training curricula.
>
> Source: Wallonia (2018), "Peer Learning in Regions in industrial transition: Workshops good practice template", Le Forem, the Public Employment Service, Prepared for the Peer Learning in Regions in Industrial Transition Workshop "Preparing Jobs of the Future", 8-9 March 2018, Brussels, Belgium, Unpublished.; Le Forem (2020), Métiers en tension de recrutement en Wallonie - Liste 2020, https://www.leforem.be/MungoBlobs/1391501709248/202006_Analyse_metiers_tension_recrutement_wallonie_2020.pdf .

2.3. Job quality: a "high road" recovery can prepare the Basque Country for the future of work

2.3.1. Digitalisation may increase non-standard working arrangements

Technology-influenced changes in the workplace are likely to create more part-time, temporary or self-employed jobs as the possibility of new, remote or modified working arrangements becomes possible. Some of these changes may be accelerated by the COVID-19 crisis as remote work arrangements persist or become mainstreamed in the workplace. Such developments could support workers who require more flexible arrangements but they could also lead to increased employment insecurity (Orkestra, 2019[8]). In the same way, technology can improve job quality for some workers, by increasing earnings, improving safety, or reducing tedious tasks. New technologies in the workplace, however, can also reduce the well-being of workers by increasing monitoring, reducing autonomy and accentuating job strain (OECD, 2019[23]). Low job quality can harm labour productivity by lowering worker motivation and by discouraging firms from investing in the skill development of employees (Askenazy and Erhel, 2017[24]).

Recognising jobs as a central part of peoples' well-being, the OECD has sought to place the quality of employment, and not only its quantity, at the centre of policy discussions on employment (OECD, 2014[25]). The OECD Job Quality Framework considers job quality can be broadly divided into earning quality, labour market security and the quality of the working environment, such as tasks performed (OECD, 2014[25]). According to these gauges, Spain records amongst the lowest job quality indicators in the OECD, a pattern followed by the Basque Country along key indicators (OECD, 2019[23]). In terms of earnings quality, Spanish and Basque wages fell sharply during the crisis and did not recover fully, recovering only partially in real terms in 2019 for the first time since 2015 (European Commission, 2020[26]). At the national level, raises in the minimum wage in 2019 and higher negotiated wages through social dialogue helped recover wages (European Commission, 2020[26]).

2.3.2. Temporary employment is pervasive in the Basque Country

Although the Basque Country benefits from a lower rate of temporary employment compared to most other Spanish regions, it remains much higher than EU and OECD averages. Indeed, in 2019, 92% of work contracts signed in the Basque Country were temporary, while in 2018, over 22% of employees were on temporary contracts in Spain, compared to just over 11% in the EU-28 (Lanbide website) (Figure 2.12). According to the European Commission, over 32% of those on temporary contracts in Spain have an agreement that lasts less than 6 months, while over 17% have a contract that last less than 1 month, highlighting the precariousness of working arrangements (European Commission, 2019[27]). Moreover, the number of very short contracts has increased in recent years in Spain. For example, 30% of all contracts signed in Spain in 2019 were less than one week long, compared to 17% in 2007 (European Commission, 2020[26]). The Commission also highlights that fixed-term contracts are not only pervasive in seasonal jobs, but also in education, health and manufacturing along with other higher-skilled occupations. Temporary contracts have also proliferated in the public sector, with over 27% of public sector employees on temporary contracts in Spain at the end of 2019, according to European Commission.

The high rate of temporary contracts in Spain causes difficulties attaining benefits and participating in training. Over 23% of workers on temporary contracts in Spain were at risk of poverty, while the share of workers suffering from in-work poverty in the overall economy increased from 10.8% in 2012 to 13.1% in 2017, higher than the EU-28 average of 9.4% (European Social Policy Network, 2019[28]). In Spain, young, low skilled and non-EU immigrant workers were disproportionately affected by temporary work and in-work poverty, compounding automation risks (European Commission, 2019[27]). The academic literature has put forth different possible causes of high rates of fixed-term work in Spain, ranging from labour market flexibility, or rigidity, to firm strategies and contract abuse. The Spanish Government has put in place the *Plan director por un trabajo digno 2018-2020*, a national strategy to curb to curb fixed-term work across the country (Box 2.7).In particular, the plan reinfroces the capacities of the Spanish labour inspectorate to identify abuses, while also opening avenues for cooperation between the national and regional labour inspectorates.

Figure 2.12. The share of temporary workers is well above the EU average in Spain, and has been on an upward trajectory

Temporary employees as percentage of the total number of employees 2008-18

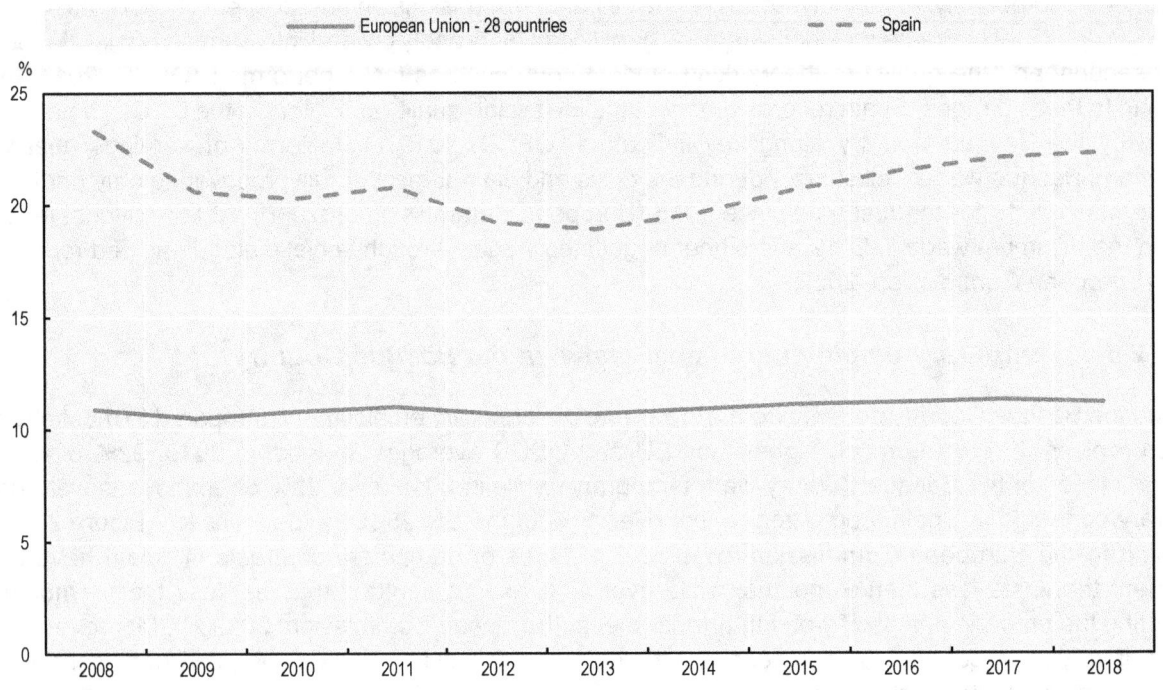

Note: Temporary employees as percentage of the total number of employees, from 20 to 64 years.
Source: Eurostat.

> **Box 2.7. The *Plan director por un trabajo digno 2018-2020*: the Spanish government's strategy to reduce precarious work**
>
> **National initiative presents an opportunity for regions to participate in curbing precarious work**
>
> The Spanish government has identified precarious work as one of the major challenges of the country's economic recovery from 2008. This challenge is likely to remerge following COVID-19. Spain has put in place a labour inspection strategy known as the Plan director por un trabajo digno 2018-2020 to curb the abuse of short-term contracts and other aspects of labour law and regulation. The plan highlights that precarious work weighs on the country's competitiveness while harming the rights of workers. Indeed, precarious work may be one of the channels for rising in-work poverty rates in the country. The plan sets the overarching objectives of improving job quality. The plan's activities unfold along four lines:
>
> - Reinforcing the actions of the national labour and social security inspectorate, the *Inspección de Trabajo y Seguridad Social*;
> - Taking into account the competences of the country's regions in terms of design, management, execution, evaluation and follow-up of measures. For instance, regions can participate in the plan through convenios de colaboración, or permanent collaboration agreements, and through campañas extraordinarias autonómicas, or target campaigns. It also opens participation to employer and worker organisations;
> - Combining short and long-term actions, including two immediate plans to fight abuses in part-time recruitment;
> - A cross-cutting approach, including 55 operative measures, 20 organisations measures and coordination from different public administrations.
>
> The plan also takes into account a gender perspective, ensuring equality between men and women are part of the labour inspectorate's activities. The plan also insists that it is solely aimed at enterprises that violate laws, and not those that meet their obligations. Some of the plan's measures include increasing the resources and capacities of the labour and social security inspectorate, using big data on contracts to identify signs of fraud, reinforcing effectiveness of the labour and social security inspectorate, greater inter-institutional coordination and a communication plan, including a newsletter, improving website information and increasing presence on social media.
>
> Source: Ministerio de trabajo, migraciones y seguridad social de España, Plan director por un trabajo digno 2018-2020, http://www.mites.gob.es/ficheros/ministerio/plandirector/plan-director-por-un-trabajo-digno.pdf.

2.3.3. Part-time employment rose more in the Basque Country than the Spanish average

Part-time employment increased significantly in Spain and the Basque Country after the 2008 downturn, suggesting part-time employment may rise again following the COVID-19 crisis (OECD, 2019[23]). Although part-time employment remained under the OECD average throughout the crisis in Spain, it increased from under 11% of total jobs in 2008 to over 14% in 2013-4, a share that fell to approximatively 13% in 2018 (Figure 2.13). Notably, part-time employment trends have been stronger in the Basque Country than in Spain, with a difference that rose throughout the crisis. Although the rate is lower than the EU average, the majority of part-time workers in Spain are involuntarily working part-time: over 55% of part-time workers were working part-time while wishing to work longer in 2018, relative to 26% in the EU the same year (Figure 2.14). Although Spain already registered a higher involuntary part-time unemployment rate than the EU-28 average in 2008, the gap between the EU-28 average and Spain has increased significantly.

Positively, the share of involuntary part-time employment as a share of part-time employment began to decrease in Spain in 2014, though this trend may be at risk due to COVID-19. As Basque firms are faced with reduced margins as the COVID-19 crisis reduces demand, particularly in sectors such as tourism, the past reaction of Basque firms may indicate a renewed proliferation of involuntary part-time contracts. In the face of such prospects, encouraging "high road" firm strategies can serve as a way to improve productivity through job quality, while encouraging firms to pool training investments, move into value added products and develop other skills utilisation strategies (Box 2.8).

Figure 2.13. Part-time contracts are pervasive in the Basque Country

Part-time employment rate, 2008-18

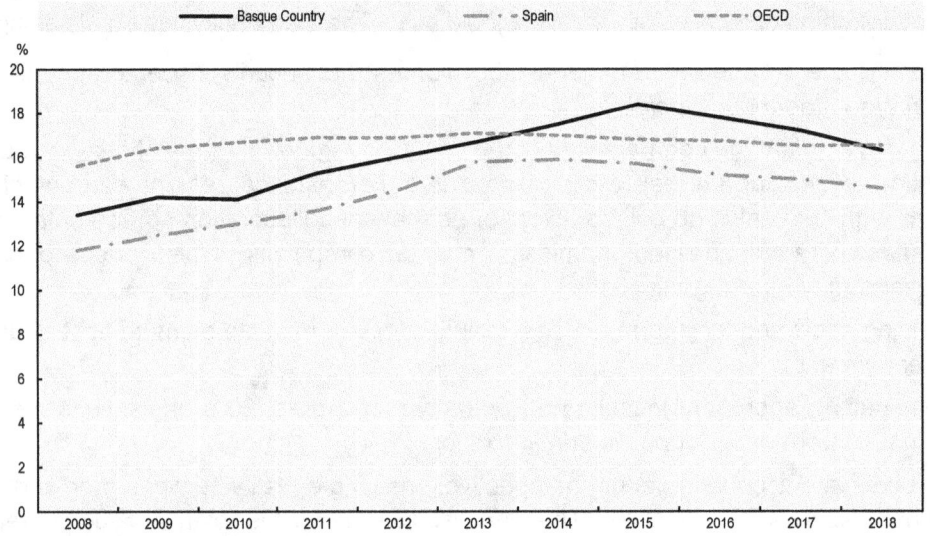

Source: OECD Regional Database and Labour Market Statistics, part-time employment rate, %.

Figure 2.14. Involuntary part-time employment makes up the majority of part-time work in Spain

Involuntary part-time employment as percentage of the total part-time employment, 2008-18

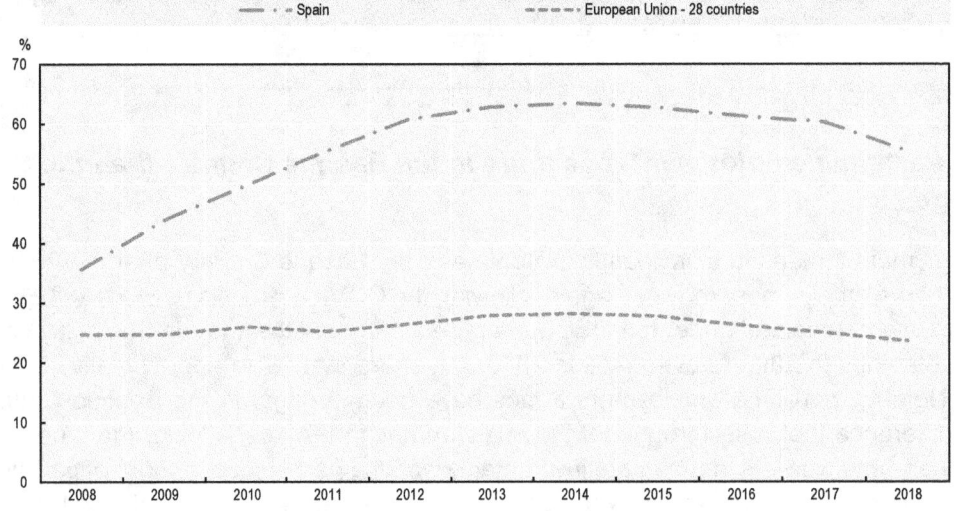

Source: Eurostat.

> **Box 2.8. "High road" firm strategies to support job quality and productivity**
>
> **Better skills utilisation can encourage companies to curb the use of fixed-term contracts**
>
> In a "high road" development strategy, reinforcing competitiveness goes hand-in-hand with working conditions, particularly through a local competitiveness strategy that stress skills development and job quality. Recent research has shown that falling job quality may weigh on both working conditions and labour productivity. Studying France, Askenazy and Erhel (2017) explain the link between job quality and labour productivity through two main channels: low job quality restrains worker motivation and reduces firms' incentives to invest in human capital.
>
> Employment and training strategies can support productivity by shaping the choices made by firms in terms of workforce composition and work organisation. The OECD and ILO have identified multiple avenues for demand-side intervention to help encourage companies towards high road strategies. For instance, governments can set "good practice" standards for companies that do not abuse labour law loopholes, pay decent wages and invest in workers. Governments can also provide funding for employers to reshape their workplaces along higher quality work practices and staff training. Other interventions can include creating programmes targeted at sectors suffering from particularly low job quality or contract abuse, for instance supporting business clusters to move into higher value added products accompanied by better use of skills. Governments can also use labour market regulations to encourage better skills use, for instance through the involvement of unions or adequate regulations on temporary contract use. Finally, regional governments can have a particularly effective role in stimulating regional collaborations between firms, creating common marketing strategies or pooling investments for training.
>
> Source: Askenazy, P. and C. Erhel (2017), Qualité de l'emploi et productivité, Éditions Rue d'Ulm/Presses de l'École normale supérieur, http://www.cepremap.fr/depot/2017/06/Opuscule_CEPREMAP43-Emploi_Productivite.pdf; OECD/ILO (2017), Better Use of Skills in the Workplace: Why It Matters for Productivity and Local Jobs, https://doi.org/10.1787/9789264281394-en. ILO (2014), Transforming economies: Making industrial policy work for growth, jobs and development, https://www.ilo.org/wcmsp5/groups/public/---dgreports/---dcomm/---publ/documents/publication/wcms_242878.pdf.

Conclusion

The COVID-19 is likely to accelerate automation in the Basque Country. In 2020, the region will face steep economic challenges, requiring the region to transition short-term economic aid into targeted support for companies and workers most at risk, particularly for sectors reliant on tourism and trade. As the region recovers, a higher number of Basque jobs will face a high risk of automation, particularly those linked to the region's historic industrial base and service jobs entailing risks related to COVID-19. These include not only occupations such as station, plant and machine operators, metal, machinery and related trades workers, but also sales workers or cleaners.

The Basque Country has already taken actions to mitigate these risks. Tools such as Futurelan can be expanded to lean on international skills mapping practices. The Basque Country can mobilise its historic cluster-based development to encourage better skills utilisation by Basque firms and acting early to train and upskill workers into quality jobs. These changes will call for effective support to displaced workers. In this way, Chapter 2 explores the way the region's public employment service, Lanbide, plays a central role support these labour market transitions.

References

Askenazy, P. and C. Erhel (2017), *Qualité de l'emploi et productivité*, Éditions Rue d'Ulm/Presses de l'École normale supérieur, http://www.cepremap.fr/depot/2017/06/Opuscule_CEPREMAP43-Emploi_Productivite.pdf. [24]

Bentolila, S., M. Jansen and J. García-Pérez (2017), *Are the Spanish Long-Term Unemployed Unemployable?*, http://ftp.iza.org/dp10580.pdf. [7]

Eurofound (2018), *Automation, digitalisation and platforms: implications for work and employment*, https://www.eurofound.europa.eu/publications/report/2018/automation-digitisation-and-platforms-implications-for-work-and-employment. [12]

European Commission (2020), *Country Report Spain 2020*, https://ec.europa.eu/info/sites/info/files/2020-european_semester_country-report-spain_en_0.pdf. [26]

European Commission (2020), *European Economic Forecast, Summer 2020 (Interim)*, https://ec.europa.eu/info/sites/info/files/economy-finance/ip132_en.pdf. [2]

European Commission (2019), *Country Report Spain 2019*, https://ec.europa.eu/info/sites/info/files/file_import/2019-european-semester-country-report-spain_en.pdf. [27]

European Social Policy Network (2019), *In-work poverty in Spain*, Directorate General for Employment, social affairs and inclusion. [28]

Frey, C. and M. Osborne (2013), *The future of employment: how susceptible are jobs to computerisation?*, https://ora.ox.ac.uk/objects/uuid:4ed9f1bd-27e9-4e30-997e-5fc8405b0491/download_file?safe_filename=future-of-employment.pdf&file_format=application%2Fpdf&type_of_work=Journal%2Barticle. [17]

Gobierno Vasco (2020), *EDIDAS programa COVID19*, https://bideoak2.euskadi.eus/2020/03/24/news_61075/COVID19_Medidas_Neurriak.pdf. [4]

Gobierno Vasco (2017), *Plan de Industrialización 2017-2020 "Basque Industry 4.0"*, https://www.irekia.euskadi.eus/uploads/attachments/10018/Plan_de_Industrializacion.pdf?1500453186. [19]

Gobierno Vasco (2016), *Estrategia vasca de empleo*, https://www.euskadi.eus/contenidos/informacion/eve2020/es_def/adjuntos/EVE2020.pdf. [21]

Gobierno Vasco (2009), *The Basque Country: Insight into its culture, history, society and institutions*, http://www.euskadi.eus/gobierno-vasco/contenidos/informacion/ezagutu_eh/es_eza_eh/adjuntos/eza_en.pdf. [22]

Hershbein, B. and L. Kahn (2018), "Do Recessions Accelerate Routine-Biased Technological Change? Evidence from Vacancy Postings", *American Economic Review*, Vol. 108/7, pp. 1737–1772, https://doi.org/10.1257/aer.20161570. [13]

International Federation of Robotics (2018), *Executive Summary World Robotics 2018 Industrial Robots*, https://ifr.org/downloads/press2018/Executive_Summary_WR_2018_Industrial_Robots.pdf. [11]

JRC (2020), *Telework in the EU before and after the COVID-19: where we were, where we head to*, European Commission, Joint Research Centre (JRC), https://ec.europa.eu/jrc/sites/jrcsh/files/jrc120945_policy_brief_-_covid_and_telework_final.pdf. [6]

Le Ru, N. (2016), *L'effet de l'automatisation sur l'emploi : ce qu'on saitet ce qu'on ignore*, https://www.strategie.gouv.fr/sites/strategie.gouv.fr/files/atoms/files/na-49-automatisation-emploi.pdf. [16]

Muro, M., R. Maxim and J. Whiton (2020), *The robots are ready as the COVID-19 recession spreads*, https://www.brookings.edu/blog/the-avenue/2020/03/24/the-robots-are-ready-as-the-covid-19-recession-spreads/?preview_id=791044. [14]

Nedelkoska, L. and G. Quintini (2018), "Automation, skills use and training", *OECD Social, Employment and Migration Working Papers*, No. 202, OECD Publishing, Paris, https://dx.doi.org/10.1787/2e2f4eea-en. [10]

OECD (2020), *Coronavirus (COVID-19)From pandemic to recovery: Local employment and economic development*, https://read.oecd-ilibrary.org/view/?ref=130_130810-m60ml0s4wf&title=From-pandemic-to-recovery-Local-employment-and-economic-development. [1]

OECD (2020), *Country Policy Tracker, Spain (updated 1 June 2020)*, http://www.oecd.org/coronavirus/fr/. [3]

OECD (2019), *OECD Employment Outlook 2019*, OECD Publishing, Paris, https://dx.doi.org/10.1787/9ee00155-en. [23]

OECD (2018), *Job Creation and Local Economic Development 2018: Preparing for the Future of Work*, OECD Publishing, Paris, https://dx.doi.org/10.1787/9789264305342-en. [18]

OECD (2018), *Productivity and Jobs in a Globalised World: (How) Can All Regions Benefit?*, OECD Publishing, Paris, http://dx.doi.org/10.1787/9789264293137-e. [9]

OECD (2014), *Employment Outlook*, https://www.oecd-ilibrary.org/docserver/empl_outlook-2014-en.pdf?expires=1576750060&id=id&accname=ocid84004878&checksum=08CD510F15872539BCF15C239C6F668D. [25]

Orkestra (2019), *El futuro del empleo en la CAPV*. [15]

Orkestra (2019), *The Basque Country Competitiveness Report 2019: Are skills the panacea?*. [8]

Özgüzel, C., P. Veneri and R. Ahrend (2020), *Potential for remote working across different places, VOX EU CEPR*, https://voxeu.org/article/potential-remote-working-across-different-places. [5]

UNIDO (2017), *Accelerating clean energy through Industry 4.0: Manufacturing the next revolution*, https://www.unido.org/sites/default/files/2017-08/REPORT_Accelerating_clean_energy_through_Industry_4.0.Final_0.pdf. [20]

3. Designing responsive employment services to help people into good jobs

Lanbide, the employment service of the Basque Country, Spain, is at the centre of the region's COVID-19 response. Established in 2011, Lanbide has a comprehensive number of responsibilities that range from managing active labour market programmes to administering the region's main income support scheme, the *Renta Garantia de Ingresos (RGI)*. This chapter looks at the critical role to be played by employment services in preparing for the future of work in the Basque Country, also highlighting new opportunities to engage with employers, digitalise services and match training programmes with job seeker profiles.

In Brief

The COVID-19 crisis is an opportunity to reinforce Lanbide's role as a labour market intermediary

- Lanbide has adopted its services in light of COVID-19. In particular, the Basque PES has prioritised the rising social needs arising from the crisis, including a EUR 100 to 150 supplement for Short Time Work (STW) schemes, *Expedientes de regulación temporal de empleo* (ERTE).
- The future of work is raising new challenges for public employment services across the OECD. Automation is supressing and changing the skills required to work in certain occupations, calling for employment services to handle more complex job transitions. Digitalisation, meanwhile, is facilitating the development of new forms of work, such as platform and remote work. The COVID-19 crisis is likely to accelerate these trends as teleworking may endure for certain jobs, and companies automate production processes faced with reduced margins. Public employment services will need to reinforce the digital training of their staff and of job seekers, while service digitalisation is an opportunity to refine job matching, quicken uptake and devote more face time to vulnerable job seekers and employers.
- Lanbide delivers a range of both active and passive measures. The Basque Country spends 1.3% of its GDP on labour market programmes. Approximately 55% is devoted to passive support, while the remaining 45% is geared to active labour market programmes. Lanbide administers a wide array of programmes for specific groups, including eleven specific programmes for youth.
- In 2012, Lanbide took over the management of the *Renta Garantia de Ingresos* (RGI), a core income maintenance programme in the region. Lanbide staff devote a large share of their time on the administration of this benefit. Despite increasing staff, front line staff face a caseload of one PES staff member to 427 unemployed jobseekers, compared to below 100 in European countries such as Germany, Norway and Switzerland. This may prevent staff from fully carrying out active labour market programmes in the region.
- Lanbide engages with employers to identify future labour market developments and control job quality. Many employers, however, may turn to Lanbide predominantly for employment incentives, without perceiving the advisory role Lanbide can play to help them best use the skills of local job seekers. In Australia, employer services staff engage in reverse marketing to help employers formulate job positions that are not published yet and that employers who might not be fully aware they need. In Germany, the *Bundesagentur* helps SMEs set up vacancies or administer other human resource services. The German PES also trains specialised staff to assist in the placement of apprentices, working with both employers and new labour market entrants.

Introduction

The Basque Country's Public Employment Service (PES), Lanbide has been on the frontline of the COVID-19 crisis. Across the OECD, PES have had to take measures to face a high intake of jobseekers and a shrinking number of job offers, while transitioning short term support into medium and long-term recovery strategies (OECD, 2020[1]). In order to take stock of Lanbide's coming role in this recovery, this chapter is divided into two parts. Section 3.1 will analyse Lanbide's role on the Basque labour market, while section 3.2 presents the opportunities the Basque PES can seize as the region recovers.

3.1. Lanbide has developed its capacities significantly to face the future of work

3.1.1. While Lanbide has prioritised needed income maintenance during COVID, it had been digitalising services prior to the crisis

In 2008, the Basque government created Lanbide, the Basque public employment service (PES), with a focus on helping large cohorts of unemployed people back into employment due to the 2008 economic crisis. Lanbide allows the Basque Country to respond to labour market needs in locally sensitive manner, reflecting the Basque Country's autonomous competencies in social and employment policy. Among a host of competencies, Lanbide provides regionally tailored active labour market policies, while also administering both regional and national passive policies. While other regions of Spain negotiate their annual budgets for labour market policy with the national public employment service, the Basque Country finances labour market policy with its own budget due to its autonomous legal status.

As lockdown measures were put in place in March 2020, Lanbide took on a renewed crisis management role. Lanbide handled an initial surge of Short Term Work (STW) schemes, adjusting its service to prioritise disbursing aid and protecting jobs. In this way, Lanbide has followed the actions of PES across the OECD. Practice sharing could help Lanbide maintain a greater array of activities during COVID, while also sharing its effective practices (Box 3.1). For instance, as part of the Basque government's emergency response, Lanbide complemented STW, with EUR 100 to 150 for those with low incomes. Lanbide also began implementing the Spanish government's *Ingreso Minimo Vital* (IMV), a minimum social revenue launched in June 2020. The IMV functions as a complementary income maintenance programme to the Basque *Renta Garantia de Ingresos* (RGI), also administered by Lanbide: qualifying beneficiaries may receive both schemes complementarily, without cumulating them (Bernal, 2020[2]). As criteria differ for reception, particularly concerning residency and wealth, the schemes are likely to target partially different groups.

Prior to COVID-19, as employment continued to recover from the surge of unemployment in 2008-2010, Lanbide was adjusting its strategy from dealing primarily with a large cohort of unemployed people to working on improving the quality of jobs and assisting those with complex employment barriers. In doing so, Lanbide had also taken steps to adapt its service to the future of work. Indeed, a host of labour market trends are inciting PES to adapt, including more complex labour market transitions, a digitalised economy and cooperation with new labour market actors. The mass adoption of remote work in the face of COVID-19 has helped accelerate the need to digitalise services. As part of multiple efforts, Lanbide has put in place tools such as Futurelan, anticipating which jobs are likely to face displacement, and has been working proactively with employers.

The Basque government also introduced a bill that aims to strengthen the role of Lanbide as a provider of employment services. The *Anteproyecto de Ley/2019 del Sistema Vasco de Empleo y de* Lanbide-*Servicio Vasco de Empleo* defines its main objectives to increase the quality of labour market programmes, the empowerment of jobseekers to find jobs, the development of the region's economy and care for the most vulnerable individuals in the labour market. In the bill, Lanbide will to lead an integrated service provision that coordinates vocational guidance, training, job intermediation, employer engagement, promotion of entrepreneurship and self-employment as well as more comprehensive use of labour market information and foresights exercises.

> **Box 3.1. How are employment services across the OECD responding to COVID-19?**
>
> Public employment services (PES) are playing a central role in the COVID-19 crisis, ensuring labour market policies are administered. PES have had to adapt to an unprecedented intake of job seekers, without the possibility of in-person contact in many countries, and with a lower number of job openings to offer. Across OECD countries, PES have had to adjust to the urgency of the short-term situation, often focusing on social support and quickly digitalising services, while preparing for the post-COVID labour market.
>
> Although significant cross-national differences exist, PES have often administered short-time work schemes (STW) to mitigate the initial increase of unemployed people. For example, Italy expanded STW availability to all sectors, while Germany increased staff processing STW by a factor of fourteen relative to normal. Social benefits such as unemployment benefits have also been streamlined, prioritising online procedures unless individuals do not have internet access. It is important PES ensure that special services are provided to those with limited digital literacy or without internet access. Similarly, job search requirements have been relaxed across OECD countries. For example, France and Germany both suspended sanctions for not demonstrating active job search. PES have switched all of their services online in an unprecedented short time.
>
> PES have also begun preparing job seekers for the labour market after COVID-19. Training has played a role in these services, as PES have digitalised training courses on a large scale. For example, France created an "Emploi Store" with more than 150 new training courses. PES have also needed to train and inform their staff on new methods of work, for instance on clear guidelines on how to perform new tasks, particularly working from home. The OECD has also identified that PES can benefit from planning exit strategies from the crisis. These can include a wide range of issues, including budgets increases needed to ensure service continuity, while also reinforcing digital strategies.
>
> Source: (OECD, 2020[1])

3.1.2. Lanbide administers one of the region's main social protection programmes

Lanbide is responsible for administering the Basque Country's main social insurance programme, the *Renta Garantia de Ingresos* (RGI). The RGI has been a substantial policy for reducing poverty in the Basque Country. The RGI was introduced in 1989 through a government initiative to fight poverty in the region. In this latest modification, the administration of RGI was transferred to Lanbide from local councils. RGI payments are determined according to multiple criteria[1]. The amount of the benefit depends on monthly income and family size. RGI functions as income support for households without income, those with low income that work and retirees who require an income complement. Payments in 2019 ranged from 694 EUR for one person without income to 985 EUR for a three-person household. Lone parents receive a 50 EUR supplement. In 2019, EUR 489,26 million was allocated to 52 455 recipients of RGI, which is 8.7% less recipients than in 2018, and 21% less than at its peak in 2015 (Gabinete técnico de Lanbide, 2019[3]).

3.1.3. The region devotes a comparable share of funds to labour market programmes compared to countries in western Europe

Employment services in the Basque country benefit from strong investment compared to OECD averages. The Basque Country spends around 1.3% of its GDP on labour market policies (Figure 3.1). This places the region among OECD countries such as Germany, Italy and Denmark if taken as a percentage of GDP.

Concerning labour market spending, the Basque Country devotes approximately 41% of if budget on active labour market measures, while the remaining 59% is spent on passive measures, such as benefits and other income supports. This is relatively similar to other public employment services within the OECD, who tend to spend a larger share of their spending on passive measures. Compared to Spain, however, the region spends a smaller share of expenditure-to-GDP on labour market policies, and a higher share on activation policies.

Expenditures of labour market programmes have also increased. Since 2013, the expenditure on active labour market programmes has grown around 5% annually, indicating that activation is a priority of the Basque government. Lanbide's strategy is anchored in the Basque Employment Plan, the *Estrategia Vasca de Empleo* and Lanbide's 2017-2020 strategy (Gobierno Vasco, 2017[4]). The region's labour market strategy emphasises labour market activation, but also focuses on increasing the quality of jobs (Gobierno Vasco, 2016[5]).

Figure 3.1. The Basque Country devotes a similar amount of financial resources to labour market policies as west European countries

Expenditure as a percentage of GDP, 2017

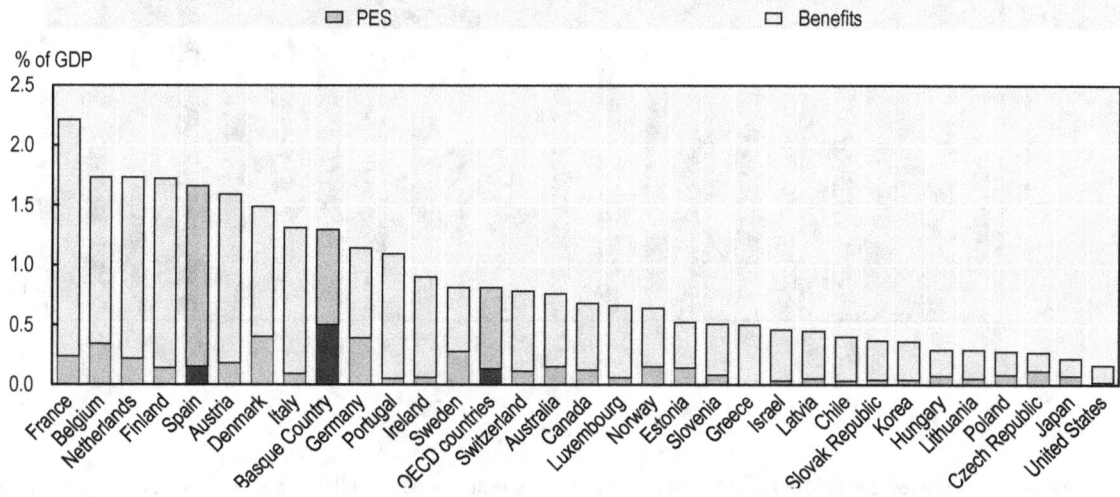

Note: PES: Public employment service. Passive policies (benefits) include expenditure on income maintenance and early retirement. There is no PES data for Greece, data for Italy is 2015. See Grubb and Puymoyen (2008) "Long time series for public expenditure on labour market programmes", OECD Social, Employment and Migration Working Papers, No. 73, https://doi.org/10.1787/230128514343 for more details on categories. Data for Basque Country PES is from LANBIDE, data for Basque Country Benefits is from the European Labour Force Survey (person is Spanish national and is receiving benefits or assistance).
Source: Public expenditure and participant stocks on LMP Dataset, http://stats.oecd.org//Index.aspx?QueryId=8540. Data for Basque Country from LANBIDE and calculations based on EULFS.

3.1.4. Lanbide reaches a high proportion of the region's unemployed, reinforcing the reach of its programmes

Since 2011, a growing proportion of unemployed people have registered in the PES in the Basque Country. The proportion of registered unemployed is a key number in labour market policy, as it helps determine the reach of programmes, as those registered can be reached by PES services. In 2018, Lanbide's registered 89% of all unemployed, placing Lanbide's coverage higher than OECD countries with highest coverage rates, such as Germany or Belgium. (Figure 3.2). It is also 8% higher than the average coverage rate across Spain.[2] A growing proportion of the long-term unemployed have registered in Lanbide offices, reaching 90.0% in 2018 compared to 85.9% in Spain (Figure 3.3). This number has risen by over 17 percentage points since Lanbide's creation in 2008, when the Basque PES registered 72.2% of the long-term unemployed. This registration level has been above the Spanish average since 2010. This high rate translates into the potential for more inclusive labour market policies, as passive and active measures are able to reach a greater number of those most excluded from the labour market. Lanbide's high rate for both unemployed and long-term unemployed people reflects effective outreach and registration strategies. The high registration rate is an asset as the Basque Country advances its COVID-19 recovery, because the PES' strategies are well placed to reach new groups of job seekers.

Figure 3.2. Lanbide ranks among the top in registering unemployed jobseekers compared to all available OECD averages, 2018

Registered unemployed from all unemployed in selected OECD European countries

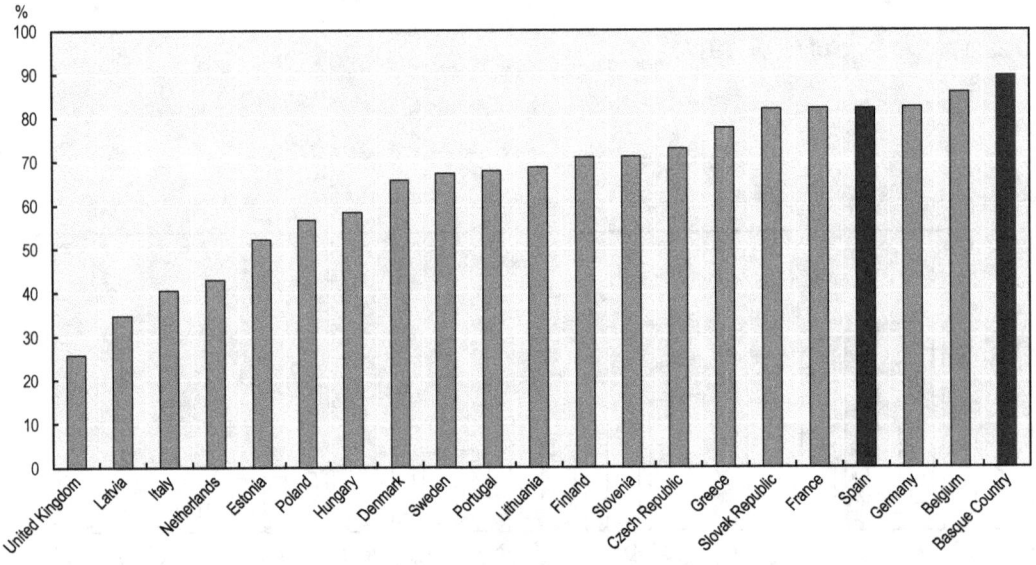

Note: The share of registered unemployed is obtained from micro data, using as base all those who are unemployed according to the ILO definition.
Source: OECD calculations based on data from the European Labour Force Survey and Eurostat.

Figure 3.3. Since taking over responsibilities for employment services, Lanbide also registers a high proportion of long term unemployed people

Registered long-term unemployed as a share of all long-term unemployed, 2008-18.

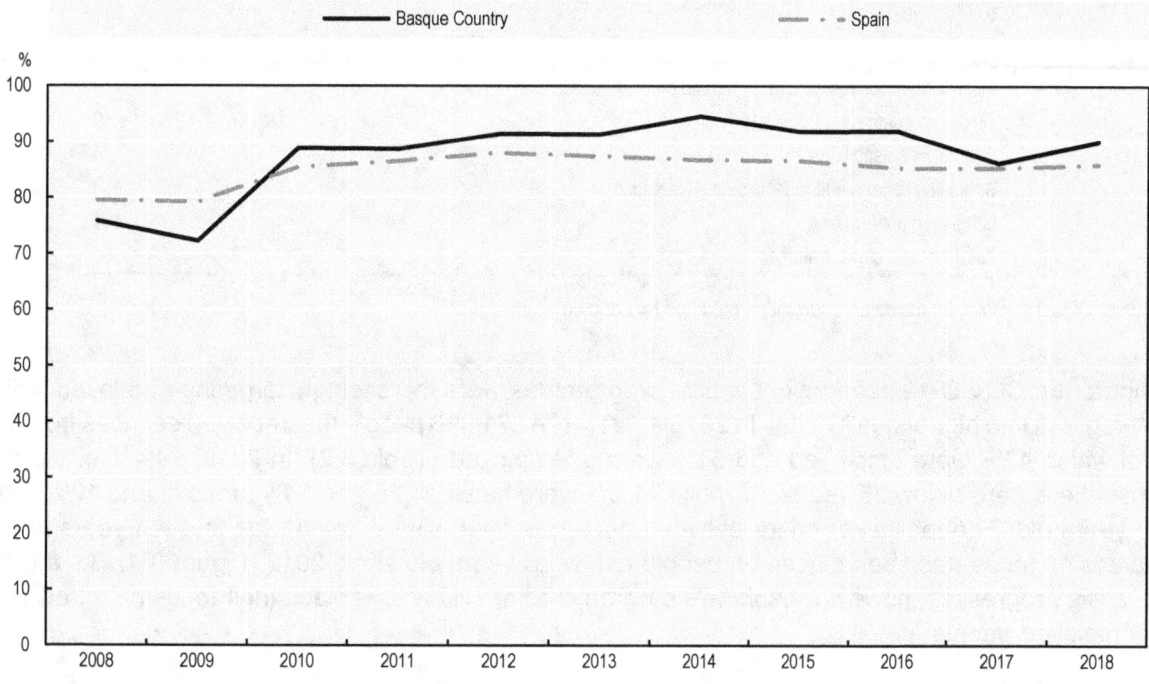

Note: The share of registered unemployed is obtained from micro data, using as base all those who are unemployed according to the ILO definition.
Source: OECD calculations based on data from the European Labour Force Survey.

3.1.5. Lanbide has developed a wide range of programmes tailored to the needs of different groups

Lanbide currently oversees a portfolio of 65 activation and job stimulation measures. While the majority of programmes are focused on the unemployed, there is also a strong focus on specific sub-population groups with lower labour force participation rates. This includes young people and women, for which eleven specific programmes have been introduced respectively to target each group (Table 3.1). These programmes will serve a particularly helpful role as young people and women are amongst those most likely to be impacted by COVID-19. Lanbide's programmes could help prevent long-term scarring effects, in which those most vulnerable face long-term discouragement and difficulties integrating the labour market. The relatively high number of programmes for youth reflects the very high proportion of unemployed youth in the region following the 2008 and 2010 crises. Moreover, specific programmes have also been put in place for victims of domestic abuse or crime and other vulnerable groups, who have had access to ten different targeted programmes. Groups such as the long-term unemployed and people with disabilities, however, received a lower diversity of programme offerings, benefiting from only one and four programmes respectively.

Table 3.1. Outside of the unemployed, young people and women are the focus of many Lanbide employment programmes

Number of Lanbide programmes by target group

Group	Number of programmes
Unemployed (30 years and over), including entrepreneurship programmes	16
Youth	11
Women	11
Victims domestic abuse and crime and other groups	10
Other programmes	9
People with disabilities	4
Subsidies to firms and other job creation schemes	3
Long-term unemployed	1
Total number of programmes	65

Source: OECD elaboration based on information provided by Lanbide

Prior to the COVID-19 pandemic, Lanbide programmes were increasingly targeting employed individuals to progress into higher quality jobs. In 2019, there were 371 896 people that received services from Lanbide – of which 49% were employed and 51% were unemployed (Table 3.2). In 2019, 14.4% of the serviced jobseekers were below 25 years old, while 71.8% were between 25 and 54 years old, and 12% were over 55 years old. The jobseeker share between ages has been similar during the last ten years, though an increasing focus has been places on people below 25 years old since 2012 (Figure 3.4). As the COVID-19 crisis progresses, however, Lanbide's programmes are likely to replace their focus on a new cohort of unemployed people.

Table 3.2. Lanbide services reach both employed and unemployment people in the labour market

Year	Number of people who receive Lanbide service	Employed jobseekers	Unemployed	People who received services or programmes	Number of services
2011	337 666	NA	NA	100 528	275 650
2012	364 496	NA	NA	125 096	420 222
2013	378 646	135 369	243 277	113 559	385 842
2014	391 099	163 310	227 789	152 116	587 767
2015	400 067	188 997	211 070	153 039	634 280
2016	401 429	195 864	205 565	128 006	452 075
2017	430 550	208 922	221 628	122 927	355 914
2018	401 576	216 016	185 560	134 704	479 415
2019	371 896	185 173	186 723	106 621	299 776

Source: Lanbide.

Figure 3.4. Lanbide programmes are reaching an increasing number of young people

People who have received services from LANBIDE, 2009-19 by age group

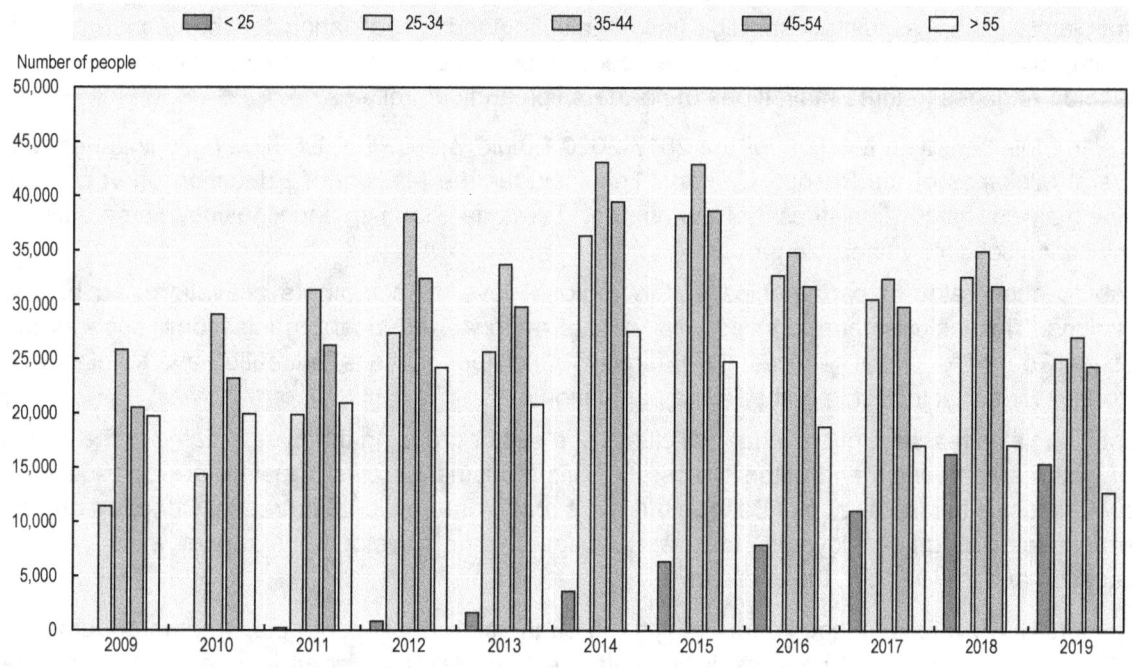

Source: LANBIDE, Servicio de Análisis, Estudios y Estadísticas del Gabinete Técnico de LANBIDE.

3.1.6. A tripartite management structure embeds social dialogue in Lanbide's programmes

The social dialogue embedded in Lanbide's management board supports inclusivity, as it allows the positions of government, unions and employers to be taken into account in Lanbide's programmes. Indeed, Lanbide is directed by a tripartite managing board consisting of government representatives, employer associations and trade unions.[3] Lanbide has three main Directorates under a General Directorate that reports to the Basque government: 1) general services; 2) activation; and 3) vocational education and training and the administration of the income support RGI. Lanbide has 42 local offices distributed over the territory of the Basque Country. Lanbide delivers its services through on-site staff, as well as a call-centre and a website to register CVs and post job vacancies. The managing board meets periodically and votes on general strategic directions and budgets. It also decides and approves changes in cooperation with public and private partners.

Lanbide also monitors and evaluates its policies through a business intelligence model. It monitors indicators and specific objectives coming from the different strategy plans and measured against achieved results. Results can be disaggregated and benchmarked on an office level. The model also includes satisfaction surveys of those job-seekers who received Lanbide services and are run four times a year. On the national level, the Spanish public employment service *Servicio Público de Empleo Estatal* (SEPE) measures Lanbide performance through the national monitoring tool, the *Evaluación de los Desempeños de los Servicios Públicos de Empleo españoles* (EVADES). Additionally, within the annual financial report for the public sector in the Basque Country, there is a follow-up of implemented activities and programmes by Lanbide and how efficiently they used the allocated budget.

3.1.7. A wide range of partnerships extend Lanbide's reach

Beyond its tripartite structure, the Basque employment service system is intended as an ecosystem of different labour market actors. Principally, this involves the Basque government, social partners, educational institutes and municipalities. Lanbide has also entered multiple public-private and inter-institutional partnerships to improve its services. Public private partnerships are encouraged in the employment plan to enhance the main strategic line of "initiating and consolidating collaboration that helps enlarge and improve the capacity to respond to the needs of jobseekers and jobseekers" (Gobierno Vasco, 2016[5]). Lanbide engages in three main types of partnerships and committees:

- In their implementation function for the 2017-2020 Employment Plan, Lanbide build linkages with several Ministries of the Basque Country. This includes the Ministry of Education on vocational training as well as the Ministries for Environment, Territorial Planning and Housing to create better social conditions for vulnerable groups;
- Lanbide cooperates in partnerships at the regional level to coordinate activation and benefit functions. This includes partnerships with various regional and local organisations, such as the Basque Council for social services, the Basque Council for vocational education and training, and a council for social inclusion of the Roma population;
- Lanbide is also reaching out to industrial clusters, a sector grouping that was initiated in the 1990s and gathers companies and actors across specific industrial sectors. Clusters are considered a powerful tool in the landscape of Basque business and its international outreach. Cooperation with Lanbide focuses on employment prospects, research and development as well as vocational education and training with these clusters.

Lanbide generally develops these partnerships through individual contracts, memorandums of understanding and other forms of partnership. Lanbide services reach different jobseekers through the ecosystem of partners and providers with the Basque Country, such as local development agencies, city councils, universities, training entities and worker cooperatives.

Lanbide is also a member of several European Union employment and labour market networks. These include the skills mobility network of the European Employment Service (EURES) and the research group European Network of Regional Labour Market Monitoring. This involvement allows Lanbide to exchange good practices with European counterparts, developing programmes based on effective practices abroad that correspond to the Basque Country's employment conjecture. Since 2020, Hobetuz, the Basque Foundation for Further Training has been merged with Lanbide. *Hobetuz* is responsible for the implementation of vocational training in the Basque Country. It was founded by a tripartite agreement in 1995 and has the objective to offer vocational training in line with labour market needs, while facilitating connections between workers, jobseekers, training institutions and employers. Lanbide's management board approves the budget for Hobetuz. (Lanbide, 2020[6]).

3.2. Opportunities for Lanbide in the new world of work

Drawing on international best practice, this section delves into how Lanbide could build on its recent initiatives to maximise its services to meet the changing needs of job seekers. The section analyses: (1) staff approaches (2) digital services (3) social benefit administration and (4) employer engagement.

3.2.1. Staff reflect an older age cohort and provide general orientation to job seekers as they enter Lanbide

Since its establishment in 2011, Lanbide has increased staff capacity significantly to meet rising demand. Staff has grown from 550 in 2011 employed full time equivalents to 1020 in 2019. Of the 1020 staff members, 73% are women and 27% are men. 60% of these full time equivalents work in employment offices servicing jobseekers, while the remaining 40% are working in the public employment service's three regional directorates. The staff working in the directorates manage the 65 activation programs communicating with job seekers via phone and email. Staff in employment offices offer also face-to-face service to job seekers and employers.

Lanbide staff benefits from long work experience in the field, though reflects an ageing cohort. 60% of Lanbide job advisors have a higher vocational education or bachelor level education, while 40% hold education attainment at lower than vocational or bachelor education. 60% of staff working with local employment offices across the Basque Country are over 50 years old, while only 1.5% of staff are under 30 years old. Lanbide's may benefit from a higher proportion of younger staff in order to meet the rising employment disadvantages of young people, in particular in light of COVID-19. In comparison, Sweden's PES has an average staff age of 47 years.

Lanbide counsellors navigate job seekers with general information and refer them to more specialised services as the job seeker's situation evolves. Across the OECD, PES establish different balances between generalist services, which help orient job seekers in initial stages, and greater specialisation upfront (Box 3.2). Job seekers who come to the public employment service to ask for support will be registered, informed about the labour market opportunities and the available support measures. The job seekers personal information and qualification background are stored. Profiling tools used during initial registration interviews help prioritise job-seekers who are already long-term unemployed or are the highest risk of becoming long-term unemployed, while also contributing to the development of individualised action plans to tailor services appropriately.

> **Box 3.2. How do other OECD employment services approach general versus specialised supports**
>
> Many OECD countries take a general approach to provide services in the first level support and do not specialize their front-line staff from the outset. Rather, they have multifunctional staff registering and profiling job seekers, such as in the Basque Country. Employment services, however, can be particularly effective when they can shift initial general support to a certain grade of specialisation when services get more complex. For example, employment services can require expert knowledge to deal with specific local economic sectors or certain disadvantaged groups. This can be done learning on internal capacity or in cooperation with an external provider network.
>
> In Europe, employment services such as *Arbetsformedlingen* in Sweden or the *VDAB* in Flanders, Belgium, have diversified their services after the first offer of support. As such, they have tasked their staff with specific parts of counselling, while automating first level support to reduce the weight of basic and repetitive questions on initial jobseeker contacts. For example, VDAB has so called job mediators who are specialised in relevant sectors in Flanders, such as construction, retail and ICT. They are experts in the requirements of the sector and supervise jobseekers and employers accordingly.
>
> Source: (Finn and Peromingo, 2019[7])

3.2.2. Digital services can complement Lanbide's generalist intake of job seekers

Lanbide helps job seekers in the region take advantage of the labour market access brought by digital search tools, without replacing conventional methods. Across the OECD, PES are adapting to the new world of work by reinforcing their digital offer while also increasing the digital literacy of staff (Box 3.3). In the Basque Country, the three most used methods for job search are convention methods, while digital strategies remain the minority. For instance, 81% and 76% of job seekers (inclusively) respectively unemployed for less than six months in the region searched for work through personal networks and ads in journals or newspapers, including online formats (Figure 3.5). Lanbide, meanwhile, is only used by between 31% to 48 % of jobseekers unemployed for less than six months, including both those who wait to be contacted by Lanbide and who contact the services, respectively. Meanwhile, between 33% to 50% of long term unemployed jobseekers use Lanbide. Digital outreach could help Lanbide both reach out to a greater proportion of job seekers while also making it more accessible.

Figure 3.5. Unemployed people do not declare Lanbide as a leading job search means

Job search of unemployed persons in Basque Country, by unemployment duration, 2018

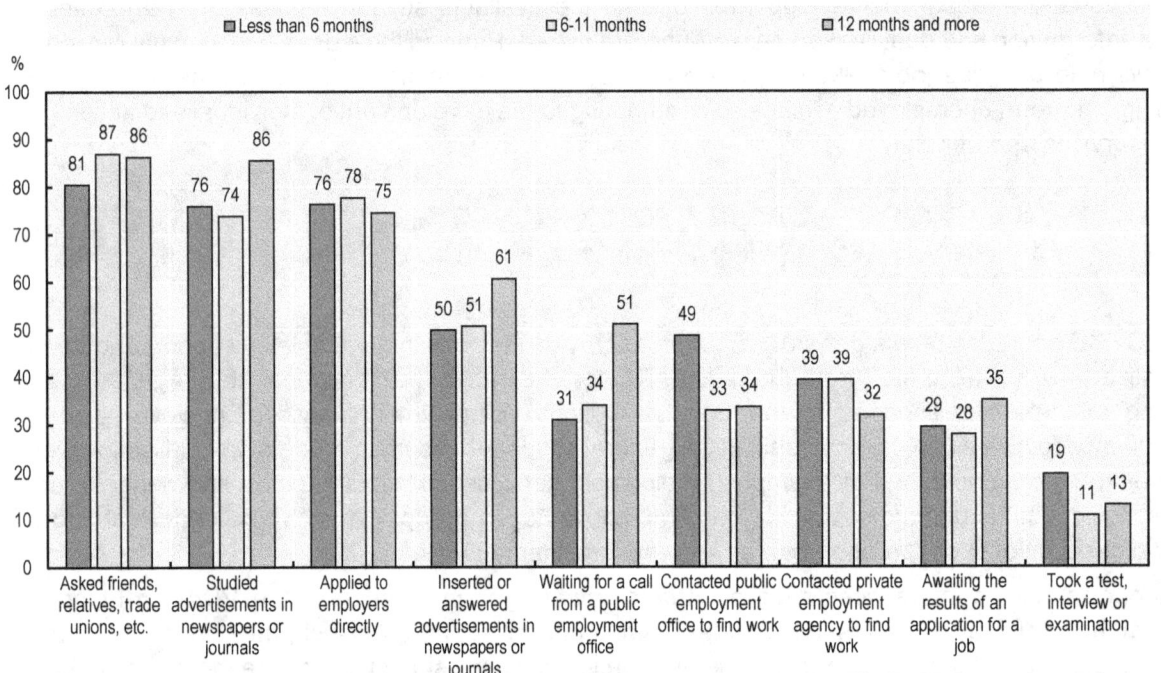

Note: The data covers unemployed persons aged 15-64.
Source: OECD calculations based on European Labour Force Survey.

Lanbide has began integrating important digital initiatives. Lanbide's reform bill envisages a digital strategy to consolidate a multi-channel approach to the job seeker search process. New technology allows public employment services to redesign processes and become more integrated, so that previously separated activities such as profiling and matching can become part of the same workflow (European Network of Public Employment Services, 2019[8]). Digital technologies can be used for standardised procedures such as initial registration and posting job vacancies; personalised interactions between PES staff and jobseekers, casework counselling functions, and skills training and development. In a number of OECD countries, online vacancy databases are the most used vacancy platforms as measured by the proportion of all vacancies in the economy being notified to the PES (OECD, 2015[9]).

> **Box 3.3. Lanbide can expand its role in a changing world of work**
>
> **The ILO, G20 and OECD have recognised the role of PES to facilitate work transitions throughout life**
>
> *The Global Commission for the Future of Work* chaired by the International Labour Organization (ILO) has recognised the role of public employment services as central actors in the future of work. In particular, PES will guide people through more complex and frequent labour market transitions. Active labour market policies, in particular, are important for better skills matching outcomes and inclusion of workers into the labour force. G20 Labour and Employment Ministers have also highlighted the importance of improving the institutional and professional capacities of employment services to ensure they are increasingly valuable in government efforts to tackle unemployment, to provide information on the labour market, improve employability and labour market integration (G20 Employment Working Group, 2015[10]).
>
> Public employment services can also cushion and reduce unemployment during economic downturns. For example, PES can provide short-time working allowances, while also tackling structural unemployment by focusing on vulnerable groups like the long-term unemployed or inactive cohorts. Changing labour markets due to automation and digitalisation require public employment services to adjust their portfolio in three broad ways.
>
> - (1) Public employment services may need to move from being mainly the fixing entity when workers have become unemployed to facilitating transitions on the labour market throughout a jobseeker's lifetime. This means that public employment services would also help manage transitions between work and training, as well as work and retirement. Many employment services already play this function because they employ counselling and career advice services alongside those staff who match job profiles with vacancies and deal directly with employers. The German *Bundesagentur für Arbeit*, for instance, applies a customer relationship-like model which puts the jobseeker at the centre of the service chain and adjusts the providing specialists around the transition rather than offering separate services.
>
> - (2) The landscape of employment services has become more diversified and complex in the digital economy. Employment services no longer manage all the requirements of job placement and active labour market policy alone, but work in an ecosystem of other actors like private providers, NGOs, welfare organisations, training institutions and industry representatives. Many public employment services are already in a good position for partnerships, since they have strong on-going relationships with the social partners, which can serve as a strong foundation for a wider ecosystem approach.
>
> - (3) Automation and new forms of work require a higher level of digital literacy for all labour market actors. Public employment services can benefit by investing in the digital skills of their own staff and partners, upgrade their working equipment and include digital skills training within a component of their activation measures. The public employment service of the Flanders region of Belgium (VDAB) has adopted technological solutions to assess and match the skills of its jobseekers and keep the digital literacy of its staff members up-to-date, while not neglecting the more traditional on-site service delivery formats.
>
> Source: (ILO, 2019[11]); (G20 Employment Working Group, 2015[10]) (OECD/IDB/WAPES, 2016[12]); (Bundesregierung Deutschland, 2018[13]) (Struyven and Van Parys, 2016[14])

Below, international examples will illustrate how Lanbide can build on its digitalisation efforts. Three transformations will be highlighted: (1) intake, (2) identification of job seeker groups and (3) vocational guidance.

Digital intake could supplement a two-level approach to services

Digitalisation is an efficient way to streamline the initial intake of jobseekers. Face-to-face entrance, however, should be maintained for those who may struggle with digital tools. Lanbide is considering digital delivery options to motivate jobseekers to register online and answer initial questions answered through web applications or in a multi-channel service approach. In this process, the first level would also have first interviews with the jobseekers about their needs as well as their sense of expectations in searching and finding a job (Figure 3.1). Indeed, the 2018 EVADES evaluation, based on European Public Employment Service Network criteria, recommends Lanbide to make stronger use of advanced analytics in the early phases of registration. Such analytics could help better classify job seekers groups, including beyond those who are unemployed (Ministerio de empleo y seguridad social and EVADES, 2018[15]). The second service level includes a deeper dive into building the jobseekers activity plan, which serves as the backbone for further employability and job intermediation measures. An important component of this plan is vocational guidance, which advises the jobseeker how to adjust the personal job profile, how to capitalize or add transversal skills and how to take local economic and personal situations into account for the job search.

Figure 3.6. Service levels for jobseekers at Lanbide

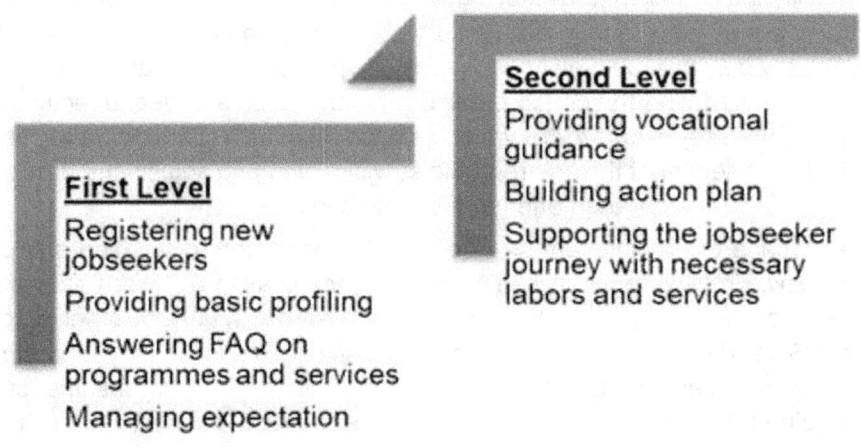

Source: OECD Secretariat based on information by Lanbide.

Codification could help record jobseeker skills in the early orientation stages. According to Lanbide staff, profiling and matching services in practice are challenging because occupations are codified through the *Clasificación Nacional de Ocupaciones* (CNO). The CNO does not reflect transversal skills of job seekers and faces compatibility difficulties with international standards like the international standard classification of occupations (ISCO) and the European standard classification of occupations (ESCO), thus complicating homogenous classification and mapping of skills. To reinforce the skills analysis of job seekers, Lanbide has been working to adjust their occupation classification to the ESCO standard. Today, after an automatised matching runs national codes through the IT system, job advisors manually revise CVs and look for further matching possibilities. In Flanders, Belgium, the region's PES has supplemented its intake process with extensive digital tools using algorithms, which register job seeker data to create an itinerary for the individual as his or her path evolvers (Box 3.4).

> **Box 3.4. Digital first at the Flemish public employment service**
>
> The Flemish public employment service VDAB offers their jobseekers a digital first entry to their services. Jobseekers are encouraged to register online and follow service offers digitally. Upon first contact, jobseekers use the "registration wizard", an AI-tool which poses targeted questions in order to register their personal situation and job search preferences. This preparatory work is stored in the personal digital dashboard (itinerary) for each jobseeker. In a second step, the jobseeker meets a sector mediator who can more efficiently help them further, thanks to their specific knowledge of the sector and the digital information available about the jobseeker. The dashboard offers vacancies to job seekers based on various algorithmic results. For example, an algorithm, known as Jobnet, matches personal history of click behaviour on online jobs against the existing vacancies of employers, generating suggestions (Finn and Peromingo, 2019[7]).
>
> In 2018 the digital dashboard handled 9 882 requests decreasing requests for face-to-face advice. On average, 38 478 individual visitors per day go to the public employment service's website, which was an increase compared to the year before. About half of the visitors consulted the website via a smartphone or tablet (VDAB, 2019[16]). A digital-first strategy, where face-to-face options remain and are even deepened for certain job seekers, are more effective at delivering employment services.
>
> Source: (Finn and Peromingo, 2019[7]).

Software can help identify different groups of job seekers, allowing for a more tailored service

Current registration at Lanbide offices already allows a basic segmentation of jobseeker groups according to their employability. According to interviews of job advisors carried out in this study, however, its delivery could be reinforced. Lanbide could look to Australia for an example of how to cater the intensity of services to a jobseeker's level of disadvantage (Figure 3.7). In Germany, jobseekers are divided into six different profiles using a software-guided assessment of their distance to the labour market. Based on this sorting, intensive services are provided for job seekers with complex problems, such as drug abuse and homelessness. Specific teams of placement officers work with these populations. Small caseloads, such as 65-70 jobseekers per officer, and relaxed regulations for jobseeker contact allows them to adopt a more intensive and holistic approach (OECD, 2015[9]).

Figure 3.7. Initial jobseeker streaming in employment services Australia

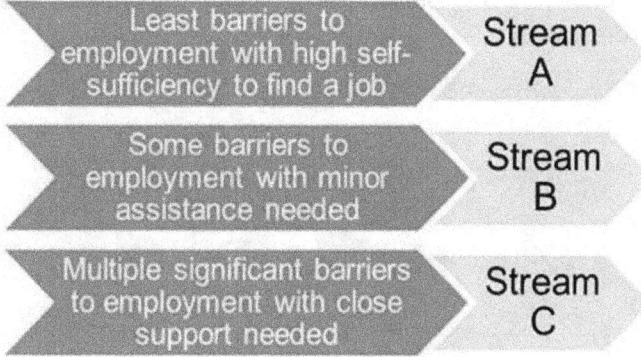

Source: NESA.

To increase the chances of helping jobseekers, databases need to centre the provided information around the opportunities of the jobseekers and the training possibilities to increase their employability. For instance, to reach out to younger jobseekers, an online job portal works best when it includes all relevant and updated job offers and CVs integrating and not duplicating other existing job portals. Matching parameters have been improved in recent years in several public employment services with the use of algorithms to support the matching and mine additional data for a more complex profile of the jobseeker. Job portals for the new digital generation also go beyond the static provision of a job offer, but facilitate networking possibilities for jobseekers, compare their trajectories to those that resulted in successful job placement and help build personal profiles through targeted CV construction. Portals can also include plug-ins to connect to social networks, create and share online content. Social networks can also be used to promote the work and activities of a PES to reach younger jobseekers.

Digital vocational guidance can connect job seeker career paths with vocational institutions

Digital vocational guidance can document thoroughly which skills individuals have as well as their current gaps to connect them to training opportunities. Modern digital job matching systems offer the possibility to evaluate, diagnose skills profiles and support face-to-face advice and vocational guidance. They also help tailor- vocational education and training measures, since they can relate skills levels with work readiness, interest in specific branches or types of work, non-formal experiences and other determinants of employability. Following generated profiles that contain all this information, the jobseeker can get personalised assessment for virtual or on-site trainings. Such digitally facilitated use of real-time information about skills needs is particularly relevant for upskilling and reskilling of adults (Cedefop, 2019[17]). Digital tools could also track and guide jobseeker careers. They can connect this information to the databases of other partners, such as vocational education and training institutions. Digitally supported training that connects data of Lanbide jobseekers can create employability accounts for each jobseeker, help the management of training centres including the design, financing and evaluation of training modules. It can also open connectivity to accreditation information of skills or even registrations and qualifications of training institutes, which would additionally structure the quality monitoring function of Lanbide in the employment service system of the Basque Country.

3.2.3. Benefit applications make up a large share of Lanbide staff capacities

Lanbide has the complex role of being an agent for labour intermediation and for social protection, a relatively unique role among employment services in Spain. This dual role is an advantage to better connect job activation and income maintenance. The decrease in Renta de Garantía de Ingresos (RGI) claimants may be a sign that some activation policies have helped RGI claimants into the labour market, while reducing RGI caseload for Lanbide (Figure 3.8). Indeed, the amount of funds attributed to RGI has decreased as the recovery from financial crisis progressed in the region, from over 507 500 in 2017, to just under 489 300 in 2019 (Figure 3.9).

| 67

Figure 3.8. The number of RGI claimants has also been decreasing with the recovery

RGI Claimants, 2016-2019

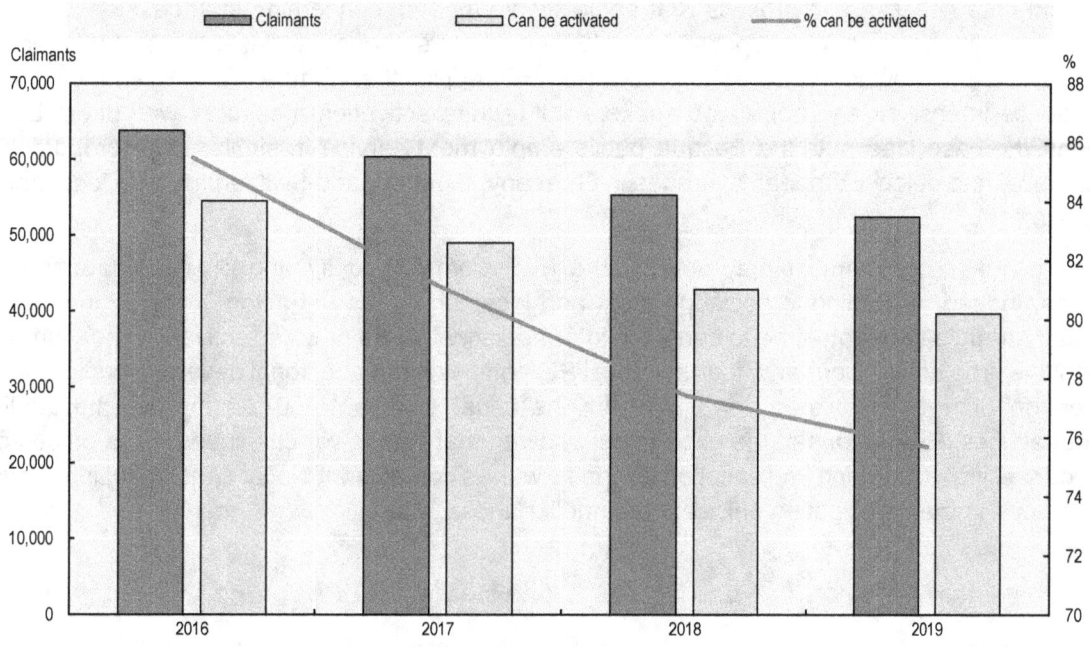

Source: OECD on Lanbide data.

Figure 3.9. The amount of funds devoted to RGI has been decreasing since 2018

RGI budget (EUR), 2016-20

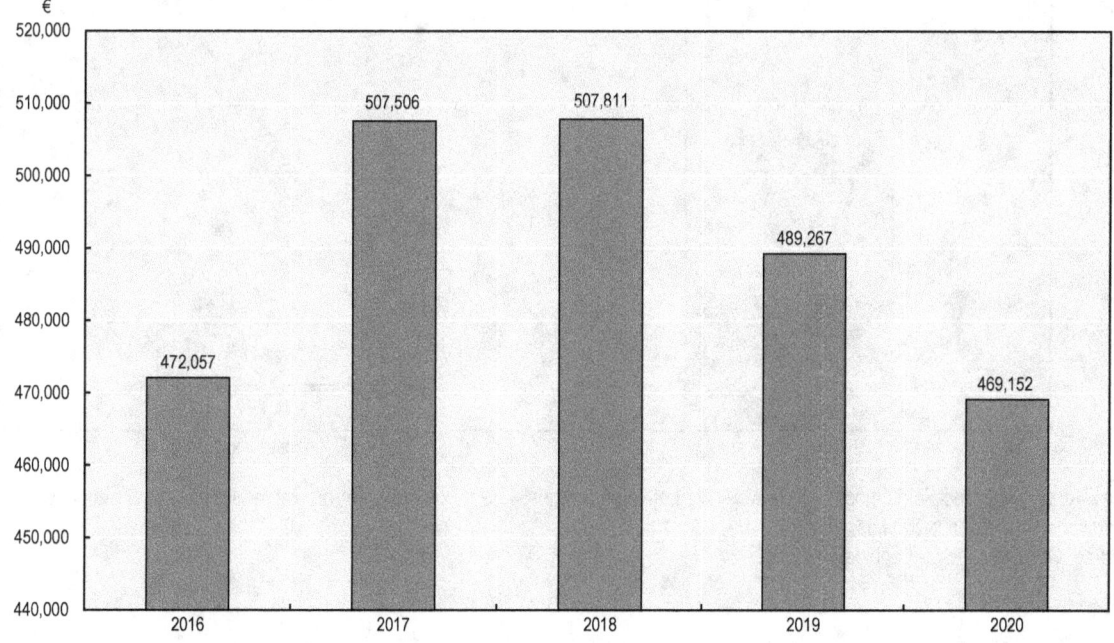

Source: Lanbide.

PREPARING THE BASQUE COUNTRY, SPAIN FOR THE FUTURE OF WORK © OECD 2020

RGI has played a significant role in mitigating poverty in the Basque Country since the financial crisis. RGI's activation arm, however, may not consistently result in long-term and high quality job placements (de la Rica et al., 2020[18]). Indeed, in 2019, only 23.2% of RGI recipients found work, while those that did tended to work in temporary jobs (Figure 3.10). One of the main reasons for low job placements may be the significant time necessary to process RGI applications. Indeed, concerning staff caseloads, Lanbide staff estimate one staff member is responsible for 426 job seekers, though representing a staff intensity of 675 when considering how long it takes to process an RGI application (Figure 3.11). Even if cases have different service intensities and not all job seekers will require activation measures with direct Lanbide involvement, the case load puts the Basque public employment service in similar case proportions as Mexico or Chile, and below European averages in Germany, Sweden, and Switzerland with less than 100 cases per staff.

Lanbide's high case commitment may prevent the PES from fully delivering on other labour market programmes. Indeed, according to social partners and local labour market actors involved in this study, Lanbide staff struggle to devote time to carry out intermediation cases or other activation measures fully. To mitigate this problem, in Germany, fourteen local PES offices hired additional caseworkers to lower the staff/jobseeker ratios to an average of 1:70 (from the usual 1:80 to 1:250) to improve the quality of placement services. Evaluations of the experiment showed that with lower caseloads, PES offices could intensify counselling, monitoring and sanction efforts as well as contacts with local firms, resulting in shorter benefit durations in the participating offices (Hainmueller and al, 2011[19]).

Figure 3.10. Few RGI recipients find quality jobs on the labour market

Labour market situation of RGI recipients following Lanbide service, 2018

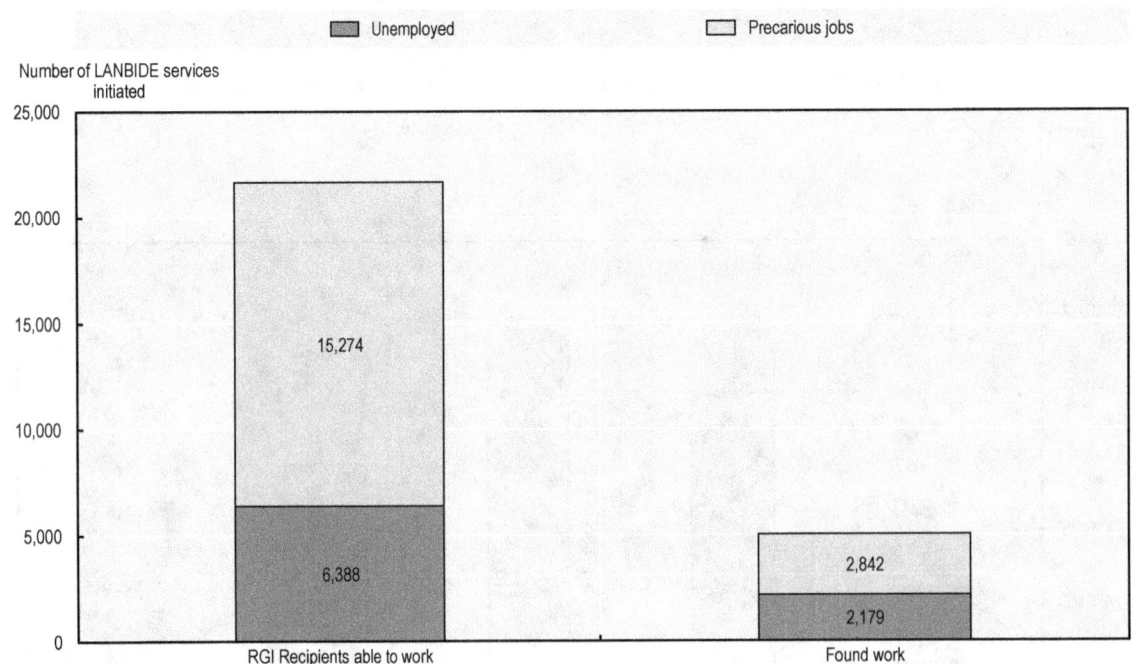

Note: Among RGI recipients those able to work are between 16 and 64 years old. Exempt are retired workers and people with severe health conditions or social impairments
Source: OECD based on Lanbide.

Figure 3.11. Lanbide staff handle a relatively high number of caseloads per staff member, as much of their time is devoted to administering RGI claims

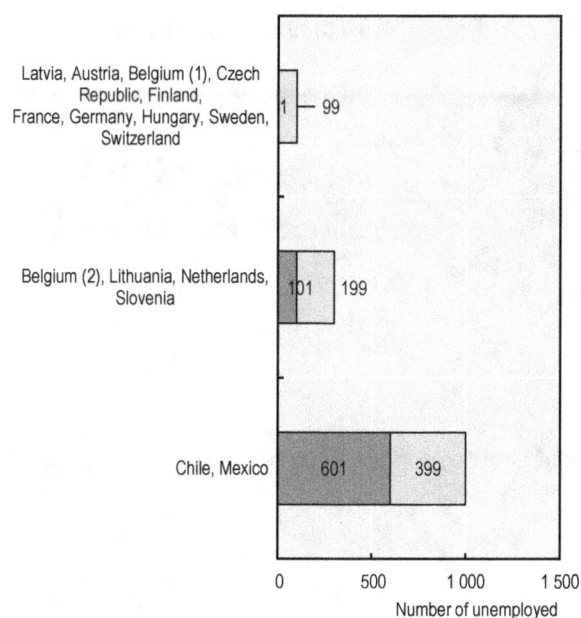
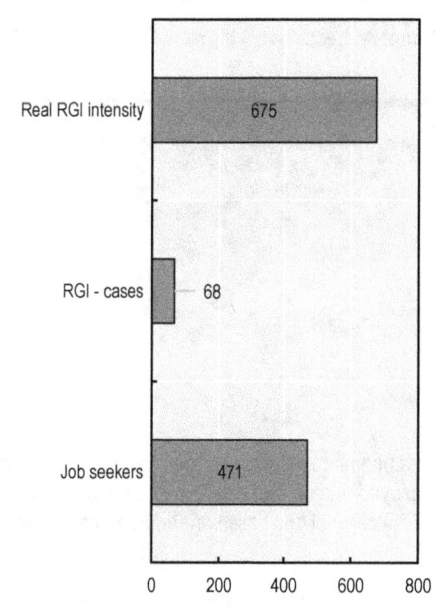

Note: (A) PES: Public employment service. Data for Latvia refers to 2016. Numbers of unemployed use the ILO definition and include both registered and non-registered persons. Belgium (1) refers to VDAB, Belgium (2) refers to Brussels-Actiris.
Source: (A) OECD/IDB/WAPES (2016), The World of Public Employment Services: Challenges, capacity and outlook for public employment services in the new world of work, IDB, Washington, D.C., https://doi.org/10.1787/9789264251854-en based on the WAPES-IDB 2014 Survey and the World Bank's World Development Indicators Database, https://data.worldbank.org/indicator. (B) Lanbide.

The lack of staff capacity to handle all RGI and activation cases may have consequences on the paths of job seekers in the region. Compared to those unemployed less than six months, a greater share of long term unemployed people in the Basque Country are registered with Lanbide (Figure 3.12). This may be due to Lanbide's strong strong capacity to register job seekers, likely driven by its dual role of registering individuals for RGI. This share of people registered receiving benefits such as RGI, however, decreases from 35% to 24% as a share of total unemployed persons comparing those unemployed for less than six months with those unemployed for 12 months or more. Meanwhile, the share of those registered but not receiving benefits increases from 51% to 75% for the same respective groups.

The pressure on Lanbide's administrative capacity may harm the long term unemployed, as they face decreasing benefits and reduced access to activation and training measures. Moreover, in 2019, the number of services rendered to jobseekers decreased compared to the year before, decreasing from over 216 000 to nearly 185 200 (Figure 3.13). This trend may have been influenced by the ongoing recovery. Similarly, over the last six years, the number of people registering with Lanbide and not gaining employment has been higher than those that are registered and did gain employment.

Figure 3.12. Long-term unemployed people risk losing benefits and activation measures

Share of persons registered at public employment office and benefit reception

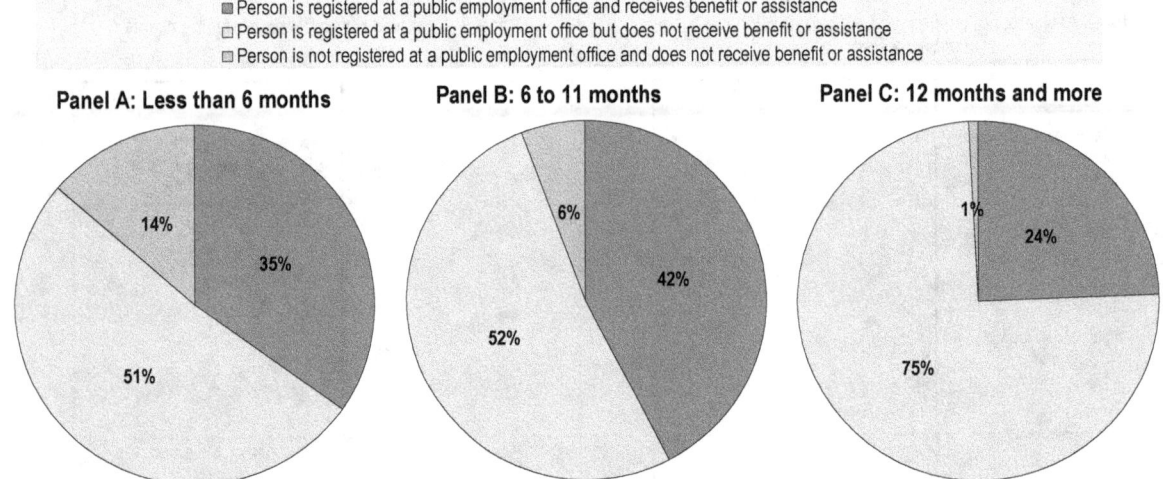

Note: Covers unemployed persons aged 15-64. Unemployment benefit is paid for up to nine months and may initially be delayed by two months if the unemployed person resigned from the previous job.
Source: OECD calculations based on the European Labour Force Survey.

Figure 3.13. There is room for more jobseekers to benefit from Lanbide labour market insertion programmes

PES registration and employment situation, 2013-19

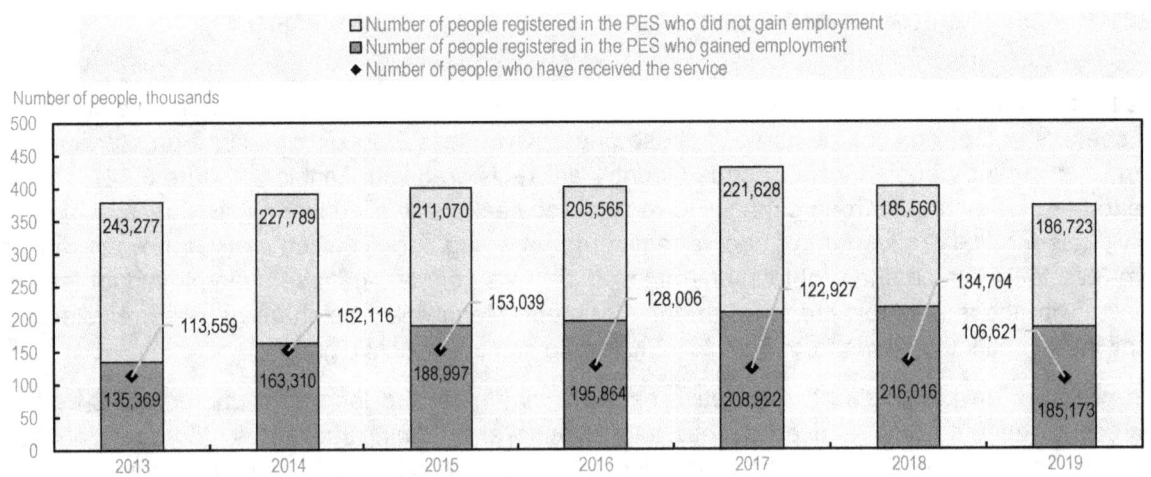

Source: LANBIDE, Servicio de Análisis, Estudios y Estadísticas del Gabinete Técnico de LANBIDE.

Administering social benefits while fully delivering activation to job seekers is a challenge across employment services tasked with both policies. There is no one-size-fits all approach. A mixture between jobseeker needs, budgetary constraints and institutional capacity is to be found. A way to reduce staff time on RGI applications without reducing coverage may be due reduce the administrative procedures required to process RGI applications. This approach may be particularly fruitful as interviews carried out for this study expressed the large amount of time needed to validate RGI applications compared to other measures. In Europe, NAV in Norway may be a relevant example for Lanbide as it covers both active and passive measures, while also adopting a generalist staff approach (Table 3.3). One way NAV reduces paperwork while maintaining relatively high coverage and inclusion is through automated services that do not overburden staff with paperwork. In this way, a more automated RGI process, for job seekers with digital literacy and internet access, could help streamline the process. In Germany, the PES adopted another approach, by separating the administration of active and passive measures, while still maintaining parts of administration. In Flanders, VDAB focuses solely on active measures and increase the agility and sector specialisation of the service.

Table 3.3. Examples of how other OECD countries manage active and passive labour market policies

Public employment service	Organisation of active and passive labour market policies
Arbeids- og velferdsetaten (NAV), Norway	NAV has a varied number of ALMPs with the aim to keeping a person in a job or giving unemployed people an opportunity to enter the labour market through a relevant programme. The NAV organisation includes the public employment services and also the national insurance scheme and the social security services. It provides both active and passive labour market measures. Front-line staff in the local offices provide services to all jobseeker groups without specialisation. However, a majority of services are offered online first. Each jobseeker will, depending on digital literacy, accesses and manages their own cases and estimate career and employability choices.
Bundesagentur für Arbeit (BA), Germany	In the beginning of the 2000s, BA linked their PLMP to employability measures by law and decentralized the services to recipients of social benefits to local partnerships of municipalities, public employment services and social support services. Like this, tasks are not only divided within the institutions giving more time to advisers to specialize on employer services or activation measures, and honing focus on local job opportunities. As a result, the individual duration of unemployment has decreased and the satisfaction of jobseekers and employers has increased.
Vlaamse Dienst voor Arbeidsbemiddeling en Beroepsopleiding (VDAB), Flanders region, Belgium	In 1989, the underlying mission of the employment service changed from payment of benefits as a supplement or replacement to salaries because of sickness or incapacity to providing an activation service largely linking access to benefits to an active job search. Within the Third State Reform in Belgium, competencies such as job brokerage/mediation, labour market data collection, the implementation of labour market programs and training were transferred Wallonia (Le Forem), Flanders (VDAB) and the Brussels capital region (Actiris) in order to enhance activation and better address the regional needs of jobseekers and employers.

Source: (European Network of Public Employment Services, 2019[8]) for NAV; (Bundesregierung Deutschland, 2018[13]) for BA; (Finn and Peromingo, 2019[7]) for VDAB.

3.2.4. Employer engagement on skills can encourage employers to better utilise PES

Employer engagement is critical for Public Employment Services (PES) to ensure job placements and support job quality. Services to employers include vacancy intake and registration, informing employers about available Active Labour Market Policies (ALMP), pre-selecting jobseekers for interviews with employers, offering legal advice and organising information sessions or job fairs. The relatively low visibility and trust that public employment services have among employers is a challenge faced by PES across the OECD. Many employers may be reluctant to turn to PES for candidates (Oberholzner, 2018[20]). Some employers may not perceive the need to address PES, or may feel sceptical about candidates sourced by PES (OECD, 2015[9]). In this way, efforts from both employers and PES can help ensure mutual benefits are derived. Below, PES strategies will be discussed to: (1) engage with employers in greater depth, and (2) how career-long career guidance and skills matching can encourage employers to reach out to PES.

Employer engagement is already a priority at Lanbide, international examples can offer avenues for expansion

Lanbide engages with employers particularly to identify future labour market developments and ensure job quality controls. Many employers, however, may not perceive the advisory role Lanbide can play to help them best use the skills of local job seekers. Facing similar issues, Public Employment Service (PES) in multiple OECD countries have reinforced their employer engagement strategies to increase their visibility.

In the German *Bundesagentur*, specific services are given to employers, especially small and medium sized firms, to help them set up vacancies or administer other human resource services. Likewise, the German PES has specialised staff members in over 150 employment offices who are in charge of managing employer jobseeker accounts, including recruitment services, post-placement services, support with paper-work, apprentice management, financial support and qualification offers. After the first contact, the employer is allocated to one account manager, who works on finding suitable skills and researching the skills market in a mid-term perspective. Job fairs, targeted site visits, networking breakfasts and dialogue with companies are standard practice. In PES branches in areas with large employers, staff can provide tailored services, such as advising companies or helping manage Short Time Work schemes (STW) during economic downturns (Finn and Peromingo, 2019[7]). In Australia employer services staff engages in reverse marketing to help employers formulate job positions that are not published yet and that employers might not be fully aware they need (Box 3.5).

Box 3.5. Building strong employer engagement through reverse marketing in Australia

In Australia, reverse marketing provides a mechanism to stimulate or define skills demand by contacting employers before they publish a vacancy. PES can use this tool to co-create job opportunities for their jobseekers close to their skills or skills potential. It also helps approach the employer with a high level of expertise in how to raise skills profiles according to companies' value chain and match them with qualified candidates. In 2011, reverse marketing made up 7.5% of the total Employment Pathway Fund (EEPF) expenditure in Australia, with around AUD 25 million (approximately EUR 15.3 million) invested into this measure and over 18 000 jobseekers profiles marketed per month.

Reverse marketing is intended to be used for jobseekers who are close to job readiness or are job ready, but who have experienced barriers to employment that may reduce their chances of finding jobs directly. Overall, jobseekers who are reverse marketed achieved 330% higher rates of job placements in the period between 2001 and 2011 than jobseekers of the same stream without reverse marketing in either the same month or the month following the reverse marketing. Proactivity towards employers can support the labour market integration of jobseekers that are most ready for work.

Source: (Australian Government, Department of Education, Employment and Workplace Relations, 2012[21])

Agile skills matching, particularly involving vocational training, can encourage "high road" firm strategies

A particularly effective way for an employment service to establish a partnership with employers is to react in an agile way to their skills needs. In this way, a PES can support the human resource work of employers, and work directly with labour market demand. By ensuring that people are in appropriate employment, and their skills are effectively utilised, employment services can promote productivity and support business expansion (OECD, 2015[9]). Given that skills needs are changing rapidly and people are changing careers frequently in their lifecycle, employment services can play a greater role in matching skills supply and demand and managing career changes.

The Basque Country is taking legislative steps to make accreditation of skills and experiences easier in the region. Special attention can go to recognising and promoting transversal and creative skills as well as digital and language skills. Lanbide co-operates with employers on various initiatives such as skills programmes with work experience components or engagement with employers to change their attitude towards employing young people. Lanbide also develops tracer studies to follow graduate labour market integration, a particularly useful tool to understand labour market dynamics. These could be expanded to support recent graduates on their first job search.

Vocational Education and Training (VET) can play a central role in this process. VET can provide training that guides job seekers directly into jobs based on their pre-existing skills. Lanbide already provides a host of training programmes for different job seeker groups (see section 3.1.5), though international examples offer paths for greater engagement with employers regarding both training and skills use. In Denmark, the regional employment services have framework agreements with trainings institutes for skills training by sectors that are in need of skills or additional certified qualifications. This allows them to offer short, modular trainings that respond to a specific employer requirement (Danish agency for labour market and recruitment, 2017[22]). In Germany, the public employment service offers a more holistic system within their dual education tradition. In particular, the German PES trains specialised staff to assist in the placement of apprentices, working with both employers and new labour market entrants. The service motivates employers to offer more training spaces to young people, so that they can benefit from the school and work in a company. In 2018, 547 000 apprenticeship posts could be acquired, leaving only 9% of the applicants cohort either unemployed or without a matched apprenticeship (Bundesagentur für Arbeit, 2019[23]).

Conclusion

Lanbide is becoming a central labour market actor in the Basque Country. Since its creation in 2008, the Basque PES has registered one of the highest proportions of job seekers in the OECD, while it has embedded itself in a host of relationships with government departments, social partners and labour market actors. Lanbide also accomplishes the major task of administering the *Renta de Garantía de Ingresos* (RGI), which has been on the frontline of the COVID-19 crisis. As a pillar of the region's social protection system, however, RGI entails a significant amount of staff time, giving Lanbide staff a high caseload compared to OECD averages. In multiple OECD countries, PES are adapting a life course approach to active labour market policies, putting services in places to follow workers and job seekers in increasingly complex work, training and unemployment transitions. To adapt a strong coordinator role of job seekers itineraries, Lanbide could reinforce its digital services, particularly concerning intake and training. Opportunities also exist to reinforce employer liaisons, assisting companies on how to best formulate offers and use job seeker skills.

References

Australian Government, Department of Education, Employment and Workplace Relations (2012), *Employment Pathway Fund, Chapter 3, Reverse Marketing*, DEEWR, Canberra. [21]

Bernal, I. (2020), *Solicitar la renta mínima y RGI: ¿son compatibles?*, https://www.elcorreo.com/economia/tu-economia/ingreso-minimo-vital-solicitar-renta-minima-y-rgi-compatibles-20200513162453-nt.html. [2]

Bundesagentur für Arbeit (2019), *Geschäftsbericht 2018*, https://www.arbeitsagentur.de/datei/geschaeftsbericht-2018_ba044391.pdf. [23]

Bundesregierung Deutschland (2018), *SGB III: Ziele der Arbeitsförderung.*. [13]

Cedefop (2019), *Online job vacancies and skills analysis: A Cedefop pan-European approach. Luxembourg: Publications Office.*, http://data.europa.eu/doi/10.2801/097022. [17]

Danish agency for labour market and recruitment (2017), *Methodology manual. Business services. An inspiration for jobcentre managers, Copenhagen.*, https://www.star.dk/media/3352/methodology-manual.pdf. [22]

de la Rica, S. et al. (2020), *Pobrez y desigualdad en Euskadi: el papel de la RGI*, https://iseak.eu/wp-content/uploads/2020/04/Informe_pobreza_RGI.pdf. [18]

European Network of Public Employment Services (2019), *Getting started with digital strategies. A starting guide on creating digital strategies for PES. European Union Publications Office., Luxembourg.*. [8]

Finn, D. and M. Peromingo (2019), *Key developments, role and organization of public employment services in Great Britain, Belgium-Flanders and Germany, ILO Geneva.*, https://www.ilo.org/wcmsp5/groups/public/---ed_emp/---emp_policy/---cepol/documents/pub. [7]

G20 Employment Working Group (2015), *G20 Labour and Employment Ministers Declaration*. [10]

Gabinete técnico de Lanbide (2019), *Informe evolución cobertura Renta Garantía Ingresos*, Bilbao. [3]

Gobierno Vasco (2017), *Plan estratégico de empleo 2017-2020*, https://www.euskadi.eus/contenidos/informacion/6199/es_2284/adjuntos/Plan%20Empleo_2017-2020.pdf. [4]

Gobierno Vasco (2016), *Estrategia Vasca de empleo 2020, Vitoria-Gasteiz*, http://www.bibliotekak.euskadi.net/WebOpac. [5]

Hainmueller, J. and E. al (2011), *Do Lower Caseloads Improve the Effectiveness of Active Labor Market? New Evidence from German Employment Offices*, http://www.laser.uni-erlangen.de/papers/paper/151.pdf. [19]

ILO (2019), *Work for a brither future. Global Commission for the Future of Work, Geneva*, https://www.ilo.org/wcmsp5/groups/public/---dgreports/---cabinet/documents/publication/wcms_662410.pdf. [11]

Lanbide (2020), *Información corporativa*, https://www.lanbide.euskadi.eus/informacion-corporativa/-/informacion/informacion-corporativa/. [6]

Lanbide (2019), *Balance mercado laboral Comunidad Autónoma del Pais Vasco. Tercer trimestre.*, https://www.euskadi.eus/contenidos/estadistica/balance_mercado_laboral_2015/opendata/Balance%20Trimestral_III_2019.pdf. [25]

Ministerio de empleo y seguridad social and EVADES (2018), *Informe resumen de la evaluación de los factores que inciden en el desempeñao de Lanbide-SVE*. [15]

Oberholzner, T. (2018), *Engaging with and improving services to employers, European Union, Luxembourg.*. [20]

OECD (2020), *Public employment services in the frontline for jobseekers, workersand employers*, https://read.oecd-ilibrary.org/view/?ref=131_131935-qg47t7rrfi&title=Public-employment-services-in-the-frontline-for-jobseekers-workers-and-employers. [1]

OECD (2018), *OECD Employment Outlook 2018*, OECD Publishing, Paris, https://dx.doi.org/10.1787/empl_outlook-2018-en. [24]

OECD (2015), *Strengthening public employment services: Paper prepared for the G20 Employment Working Group*. [9]

OECD/IDB/WAPES (2016), *The World of Public Employment Services: Challenges, capacity and outlook for public employment services in the new world of work*, Inter-American Development Bank, Washington, D.C., https://dx.doi.org/10.1787/9789264251854-en. [12]

Struyven, L. and L. Van Parys (2016), *How to act? Implementation and evolution of the PES conductor role: The Belgian PES in Flanders as a case study, European Union, Brussels*. [14]

VDAB (2019), *Key Figures 2018*, https://www.vdab.be/sites/web/files/doc/trends/kerncijfers-2018-ENG_DEF.pdf. [16]

Notes

[1] Families must be declared households at least one year before application and the residence of applicants in the Basque Country should date back at least three years. The living income complement cannot be allocated to those living in social housing or other public care centres, neither to prison inmates, while benefits apply only for people over 23 years.

[2] This proportion is calculated using the registered unemployed rate, a subgroup of the total registered jobseekers. Total registered jobseekers usually include other groups like employed jobseekers, active labour market measure participants and other groups not fulfilling the definitions of registered unemployed.

[3] Changes are adopted through simple majority of the present voting parties. The managing board holds extraordinary meetings and votes in case decisions on specific urgent matters have to be taken before the next regular meeting.

4. Skills in the Basque Country

The Basque Country has achieved a high level of educational achievement. Low job quality and the demand for skills, however, are contributing to over-qualification in the region. The region benefits from a strong VET system and a host of active labour market programmes tailoring training and labour market insertion to job demand. Firms, meanwhile, could better utilise the skills of the workforce, while adult learning could help bridge gaps between worker skills and firm demand later in life. A renewed social dialogue roundtable is supporting these workplace changes. Dual education, meanwhile, is taking a more prominent role in the region, constituting an opportunity to expand to higher skill levels and vulnerable groups.

In Brief

A high level of skills in the region is an opportunity to drive inclusive growth

- Job polarisation has accelerated in the region since the 2008 crisis. Middle skill jobs have decreased by over 6.0 percentage points, while low skill and high skilled grew by 1.6 and 4.8 percentage points respectively since 2000. Automation is likely to drive middle skill job loss in the region, while workforce upskilling and changes in wage-setting may have also contributed to polarisation.

- In 2018, 50% of the Basque population had attained tertiary education or higher, an 18% rise from the level of educational attainment in 2000. The Basque population has attained a higher tertiary educational rate than the OECD average of 36.9% and 27.3% in Spain.

- This progress, however, is not benefiting the region fully, as over 33% of people work in jobs below their education level, recording the second-highest over-qualification rate in Spain. High over-qualification constitutes a missed opportunity to move into higher level activities and raise labour productivity, while helping workers secure higher quality jobs.

- At the same time, firms are declaring hiring difficulties. In 2016, 48% of firms surveyed by the local employer federation reported difficulties hiring, a number that rose to 71% in 2018. Low job quality and mismatch are the most likely drivers of hiring difficulties, though an employer survey run by the Basque government could refine information on skills use and skills demand.

- The region's renewed social dialogue round table, the *Mesa de Diálogo Social*, is moving towards a social pact for the future of work, and creating new labour market initiatives. These are opportunities to support workers adapt skills and for firms to strengthen the quality of jobs.

- Adult learning has progressed in the Basque Country. The latest OECD survey data shows that around 46% of adults participate in adult learning, around the same proportion as in Spain but lower than the OECD average of 49%. Evidence from Spain, however, suggests adult learning funds could be better used by companies, particularly to reduce skills mismatch.

- Between 2011 and 2018, the region's VET system of excellence has continued to grow, with enrolment increasing from 34 000 to 40 000. Dual VET has shown signs of effectiveness for job placement as well as student and firm satisfaction. International examples exist to expand apprenticeships to university, while reinforcing the capacity of training centres to adapt to dual education.

Introduction

In section 4.1, the skills of the Basque workforce will be analysed, with a particular attention to the polarisation of jobs and skills mismatch. The chapter will also turn to the Basque Country's adult learning, social dialogue and Vocational Education and Training (VET) system in sections 4.2 and 4.3.

4.1. The Basque workforce's high skills are an opportunity for the region

4.1.1. The 2008 crisis likely accelerated job polarisation in the Basque Country

The Basque labour market has polarised between 2000 and 2017, a process by which the relative shares of low and high skill jobs grow, while those at the middle of the skill distribution decline. Compared to other regions in Spain, polarisation has been more moderated (Figure 4.1). In the 2000-2017 period, as a share of total employment, middle skill jobs have decreased by over 6 percentage points, while low skilled and high skilled have grown by 1.6 and 4.8 percentage points respectively. In Spain, middle skill jobs decreased their share of total employment by nearly 8 percentage points, while low and high skill jobs increased 3.2 and 5.7 percentage points respectively. In total jobs, the Basque Country gained over 60 000 high skill jobs and almost 29 000 low skill jobs, while it lost nearly 34 000 middle skill jobs.

OECD calculations suggest the Basque Country has not upskilled its jobs to the same degree as other regions in Spain. In Catalonia and Madrid, the share of high skill jobs grew by 6.9 and 10.4 percentage points respectively. The shares of middle skill jobs in Catalonia and Madrid, meanwhile, declined by 9.6 and 11.1 percentage points respectively. This trend suggests the Basque Country has retained a greater share of middle skill occupations than other large economic regions in Spain, while creating a more moderate share of high skill jobs. Evidence from Chapter 1 suggests the Basque Country has struggled to generate high skill occupations associated with the service sector. The region's Smart Specialisation Strategy (RIS3), planning investments in fields such as biotechnology and energy, may help diversify the region's employment base to mitigate this challenge.

Middle skill job loss may have accelerated in the Basque Country after 2008, before recovering. Indeed, OECD calculations complement research on the Spanish labour market before the crisis. Between 1995 – 2007 and 1990 – 2008, research has found general upskilling in Spain, including a growth in middle-skilled occupations (Fernández-Macías, 2012[1]) (Oesch and Rodríguez Menés, 2011[2]). This may indicate the 2008 and 2010 crises concurred with middle skill job loss in the Basque Country. In particular, middle skill industrial occupations where amongst those that decreased the most in the prolonged economic downturn that followed the 2008 crisis. Meanwhile, low skill job creation across Spain may have come predominately from the service sector (Peugny, 2019[3]).

Different forces may be driving polarisation in the Basque Country. According to routine biased technological change, firms have increasingly introduced labour-saving technology that has displaced routine manual and cognitive tasks (Sebastian and Biagi, 2018[4]). These tasks are associated with middle skill occupations. Meanwhile, high skill occupations benefit, as their demand rises due to their complementarity with new technologies. This may be a relevant explanation in the Basque Country, particularly in industrial manufacturing. Indeed, between 2016 and 2017, industry in Spain increased shipments of multipurpose industrial robots by 12%, compared to 3%, 5% and 6% increases in the UK, Germany and France respectively (International Federation of Robotics (IFR), 2018[5]). Rises in educational attainment may also explain polarisation, supporting the gradual growth of high skill jobs (Oesch and Rodríguez Menés, 2011[2]). Research also suggests changes in wage-setting institutions influence polarisation trends, particularly by facilitating the creation of low-paid personal service jobs, a notable trend across Spain (Oesch and Rodríguez Menés, 2011[2]).

Figure 4.1. Middle-skilled jobs have declined since 2000

Polarisation, TL2 regions in Spain, 2000-17

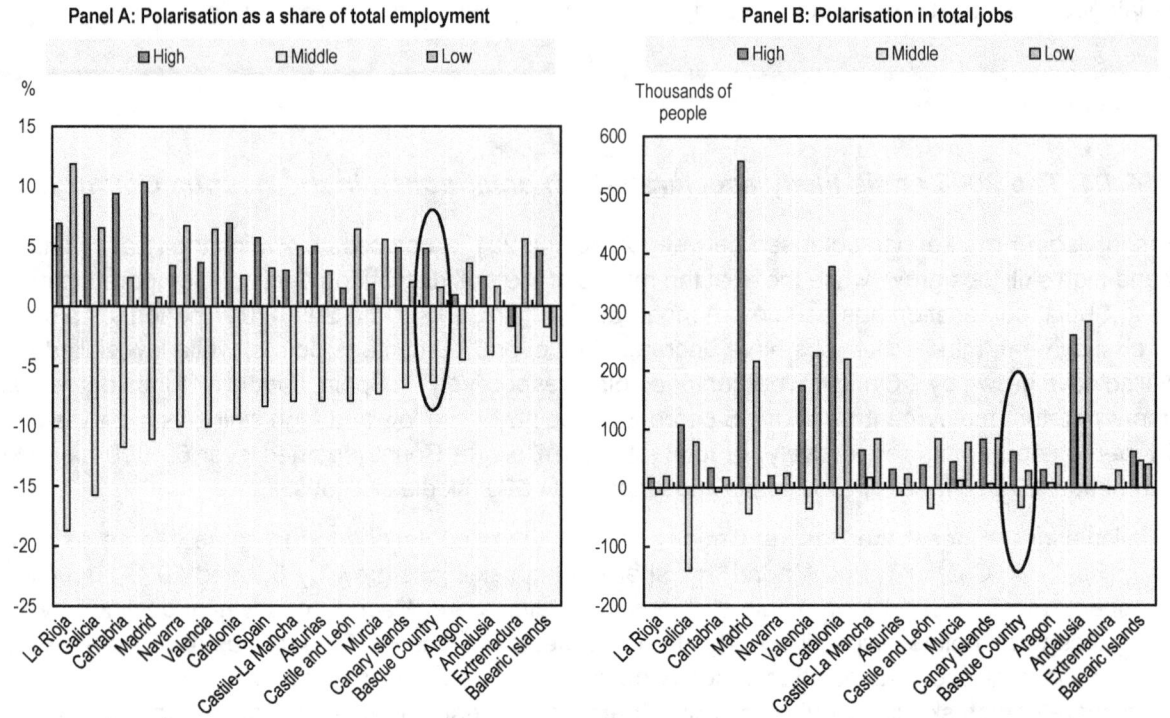

Note: Employment change in percentages and thousands between 2000-17. Ceuta and Melilla were excluded from the figures due to the small number of observations.
Source: OECD calculations on Labour Force Surveys.

StatLink https://doi.org/10.1787/888934188424

4.1.2. The Basque Country can benefit from its highly-educated workforce

In 2018, the level of tertiary educational attainment continued to increase, reaching much higher levels than the OECD. The share of the adult population with tertiary education has increased from 32% in 2000 to nearly 50% of the population in 2018 (Figure 4.2). In 2018, a significantly larger share of the Basque Country's adult population had tertiary education compared to the Spanish and the OECD average, 37.3% and 36.9%. Meanwhile, the share of the population with upper secondary and post-secondary non-tertiary education, such as vocational training, has also increased from 16.6% in 2000 to 22.2% in 2018. Those with upper secondary and non-tertiary post-secondary education, however, constitute a smaller share of the adult population compared to the OECD average of 42.5%. The Basque Country's highly education labour force corresponds to the progressive upskilling of the region's jobs, and constitutes an advantage as the region seeks to diversify and upskill its job base. The lack of quality high skill jobs, including wages and career prospects, may be contributing to a high level of over-qualification in the region. Those with below upper secondary education, meanwhile, has decreased from 51.4% of the population in 2000 to 28.3% in 2018 in the Basque Country. These patterns followed trends in Spain and the OECD, as the proportion of those with tertiary education increased by 7.9%, 7.8% and 8.1% in the Basque Country, Spain and the OECD respectively between 2008 and 2018 (Figure 4.3).

Figure 4.2. Educational attainment has progressed steadily in the Basque Country

Educational attainment in Basque Country, 2000-18

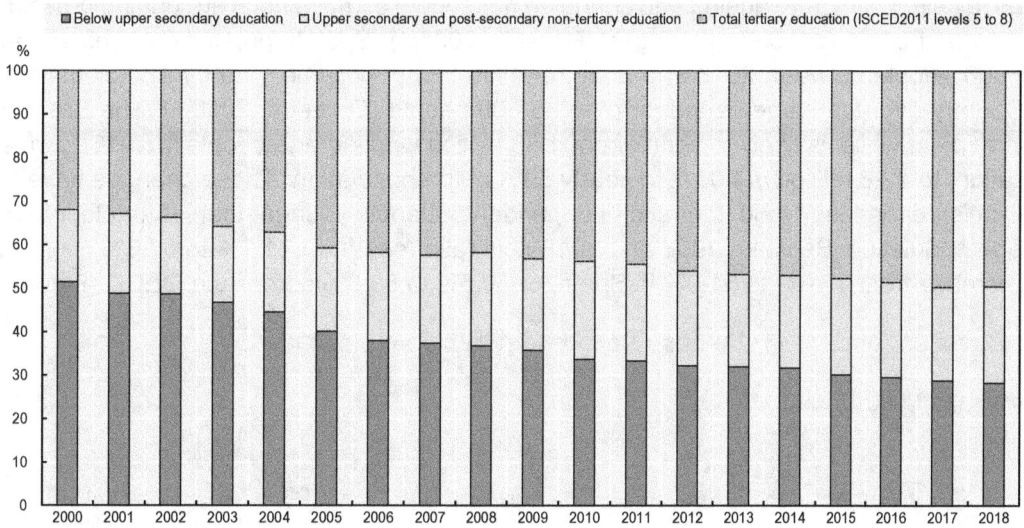

Source: OECD Regional Database.

Figure 4.3. The Basque Country has been successful at moving towards a highly educated workforce

Change in educational attainment between 2008-18

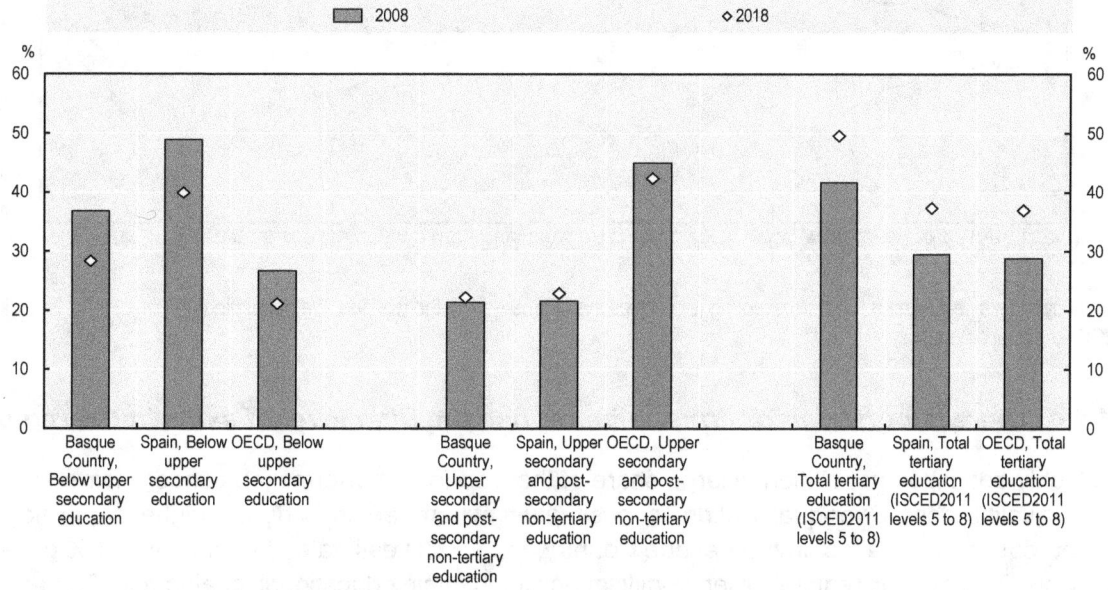

Note: Share of population 25 to 64 year-olds by educational attainment. Data for OECD for upper secondary and post-secondary non-tertiary education refers to upper secondary.
Source: OECD regional database and OECD Data for the OECD average.

4.1.3. The Basque workforce is ageing more rapidly than Spanish and OECD averages

The Basque workforce is ageing, creating an opportunity for new labour market entrants. Across developed economies, a falling birth rate, ageing and changing household compositions are putting pressure on social programmes and creating labour shortages (Pierson, 2001[6]). Spain's population is estimated to fall by over 495 000 people between 2018 and 2030, or 1% of its population, and by approximately 3% in the Basque Country over the same period, or over 66 000 people (Orkestra, 2019[7]). The Basque Country's labour force, meanwhile, is likely to shrink from 1.38 million working age people in 2016, or nearly 64% of the population, to 1.28 million in 2031, or nearly 59% of the population. These changes have put presses on the region's dependency ratio, the ratio of dependents (people younger than 15 or older than 64) to the working-age population. Between 2008 and 2018, this ratio rose from 41.1% to 57.6%, significantly more than the increase from 45.6% to 51.9% in Spain, or 50.5% to 53.6% across the OECD (Figure 4.4).

Figure 4.4. The dependency ratio has risen considerably since 2011

Dependency ratio, 2000-18

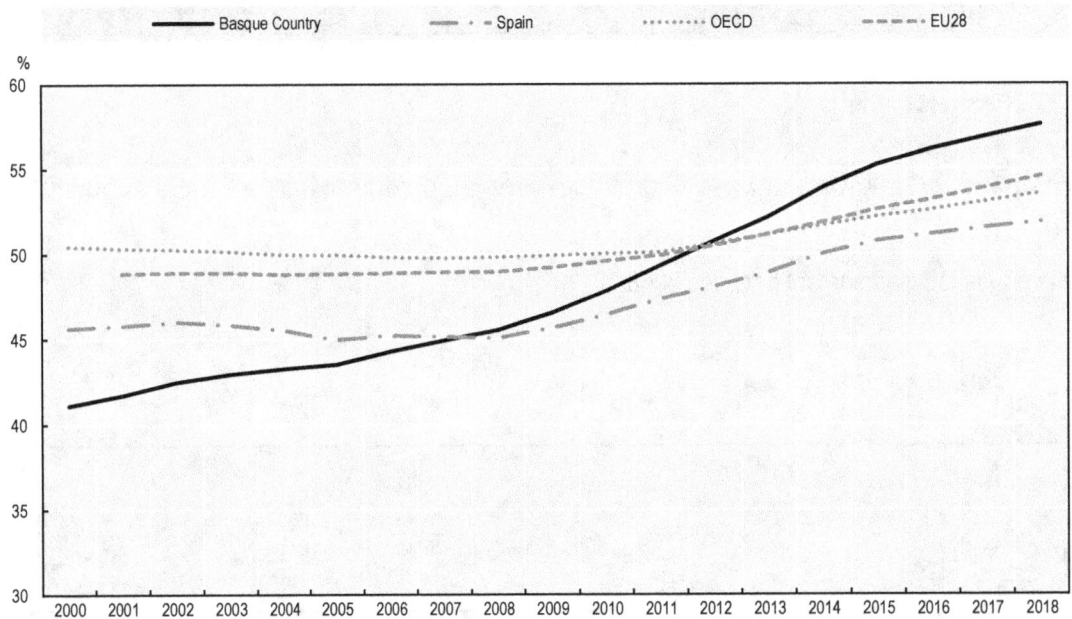

Note: Dependency ratio is calculated as a share of young (0-14) plus the old (65+) from the working age population (15-64).
Source: OECD Regional database.

4.1.4. There is potential for firms to better use the high level of skills in the region

Despite a highly education population, a large share of the workforce performs jobs under their skill level, driving over-qualification. Over-qualification is a situation where an individual's highest qualification exceeds that required for the job. In the Basque Country, the OECD estimates that nearly 30.5% of those employed work in jobs that require lower qualifications than their educational attainment (Figure 4.5). Compared to other Spanish regions, the Basque Country recorded the second-highest over-qualification rate, with only Navarra recording a higher rate of 33.6%. The share of over-qualified workers is approximately 10% higher than large economic regions such as Catalonia or Madrid, where 20.8% and 18.6% are over-qualified, and 7 percentage points above the Spanish average of 22.9%. . Meanwhile, only

9.4% of those employed in the region work in jobs above their skill level, the second-lowest rate in Spain after Navarra, where 9.3% are under-qualified.

A better use of the region's skills by firms could reduce over-qualification. The Basque Country has taken significant steps to better understand labour market needs, particularly through Lanbide, and has put in place industrial policies to diversify its economic base into innovation-intensive sectors. However, there is also increasing recognition that policy makers can look at the demand for skills by firms, including how skills are used and deployed in the workplace. At its core, skills use refers to the way that employers use the skills of employees in the workplace, and the alignment of the competences of workers to the demands and needs of the business.

One potential avenue for better skills use is promoting high-performance working practices (HPWPs) (OECD/ILO, 2017[8]). To introduce HPWP, companies can take a number of initiatives. For instance, companies can increase employee involvement in discussions of business strategy, which aims to more effectively use employees' knowledge and experience. HPWP can also grant employees more freedom and autonomy to make decisions about how they perform their job, and facilitating skill acquisition at work. For instance, in northern Italy, the OECD and ILO have documented how local firms pooled investments and shared strategies to move up the product chain, creating a demand for more specific and higher skills within the firm (Box 4.1). Worker representatives were involved to include workers in decision-making. To encourage businesses to take these strategies, regional governments can set industry-wide standards, weigh in through agreements with social partners, support employers directly to change policies, leverage anchor institutions such as training centres, support the creation of a local brand or change legislation (OECD/ILO, 2017[9]).

Figure 4.5. Many Basque workers are in occupations under their skill level

Mismatch, TL2, 2018

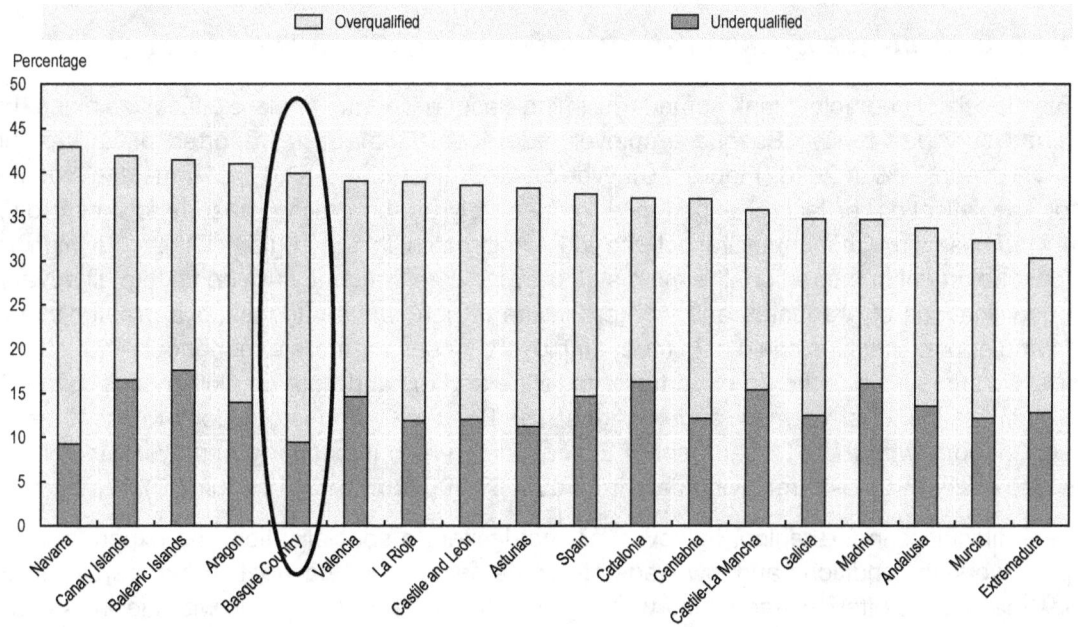

Note 1: ISCED groups 0-2, 3, 4, 5-8. ISCED groups 303 and 304 are considered to be 300 according to the newest 2011 isced classification. There is no 400 for Basque Country.
Note 2. It is not advisable to use numbers of places with less than 100k employment (Ceuta and Melilla excluded from the graph).
Source: OECD calculations on European labour force survey.

StatLink https://doi.org/10.1787/888934188443

> **Box 4.1. How local actors mobilised to change work practices in the Rivera del Brenta industrial district in Italy**
>
> **Anchor institutions, such as universities or chambers of commerce, can reach out to employers to change work practices**
>
> In the Rivera del Brenta industrial district in Northern Italy, a local employers association helped to raise productivity and skills utilisation in local footwear firms. To do so, the local footwear firm association, the *Associazione Calzaturifici della Riviera del Brenta* (ACRiB), tapped into international markets for high-quality, high-fashion, shoes. ACRiB helped firms collaborate on a common marketing strategy, while also pooling investment in training provision and helping firms to collectively upgrade their product market strategies. The region traditionally hosted cottage-based shoe making industries which mainly employed low skill blue collar workers, but by moving up the product chain, has become a global centre for the production of shoes for brands such as Giorgio Armani, Louis Vuitton, Chanel, Prada and Christian Dior. Today, design and commercial development constitutes an anchor employer.
>
> The privately-run local polytechnic, *Politecnico Calzaturiero* also played a role in this evolution, employing firm managers to train local workers and job seekers after hours, while also offering management training, and investing in research, innovation and technology transfer. The polytechnic invested in skills supply, whilst also optimising skills utilisation through new product development and improved human resource management. When firms are part of ACRiB, they are able to pool training, technology and new innovations. ACRiB has also worked in partnership with local unions to ensure that during this time, improved productivity resulted in higher wages and better health and safety for the workers.
>
> Source: OECD/ILO (2017), Better Use of Skills in the Workplace: Why It Matters for Productivity and Local Jobs, OECD Publishing, Paris. http://dx.doi.org/10.1787/9789264281394-en.

4.1.5. Low job quality and mismatch drive hiring difficulties in the region

Despite high levels of unemployment, some firms in the Basque Country declare difficulties hiring. In 2016, 48% of firms surveyed by the Basque employer federation, Confebask, reported difficulties hiring, a number that rose to 71% in 2018 (Figure 4.6). When asked, 56.2% and 52.8% of firms declared a lack of training or specialisation, or lack of experience, respectively as the driving reasons for hiring difficulties (Figure 4.7). These firm responses reflect the skills mismatch in the region. Given the high level of educational attainment in the region, the mismatch may indicate firms may not be taking full advantage of the high qualifications of graduates and workers in the region, while suggesting a greater use of dual education and apprenticeships could help meet employers' needs for more experience. A government-run employer skills surveys could be an opportunity to refine and expand data on skills needs in the Basque Country, receiving input from a wide range of firms. The Basque Country could look to countries such as the United Kingdom, where the Department of Education carries out extensive surveys of the skills needs and skills use every two years, receiving data from over 87 000 firms in 2017 (Box 4.2).

Recruitment difficulties in the region, however, are not limited to specialisation and experience, but also include poor working conditions and low wages in some sectors and occupations. In particular, Basque companies may not be offering wages and working conditions that corresponds with the workforce's high educational attainment, or may come short of paying adequate wages in lower skill jobs. Indeed, according to the Confebask survey, nearly one-fifth of firms declared the candidates evaluation of low wages as a reason for hiring difficulties (Figure 4.7). These responses also confirm responses from Basque branches of Spanish unions, Comisiones Obreras (CCOO) and the Unión General de Trabajadores (UGI), from fieldwork carried out for this study, who highlighted precarious work as a major challenge. In Spain, OECD calculations suggest the share of middle paid jobs has decreased by 7.1% while that of low paid jobs has increased by 4.6% between 2006 and 2016, greater than the 2.5% increase in high pay jobs (OECD, 2019[10]). Out of 31 OECD countries estimated over this period, Spain records the highest loss of middle pay jobs and the second-highest increase in the share of low pay jobs.

Figure 4.6. Some firms declare difficulties hiring

Firms that had or did not have difficulties in hiring, 2016, 2018

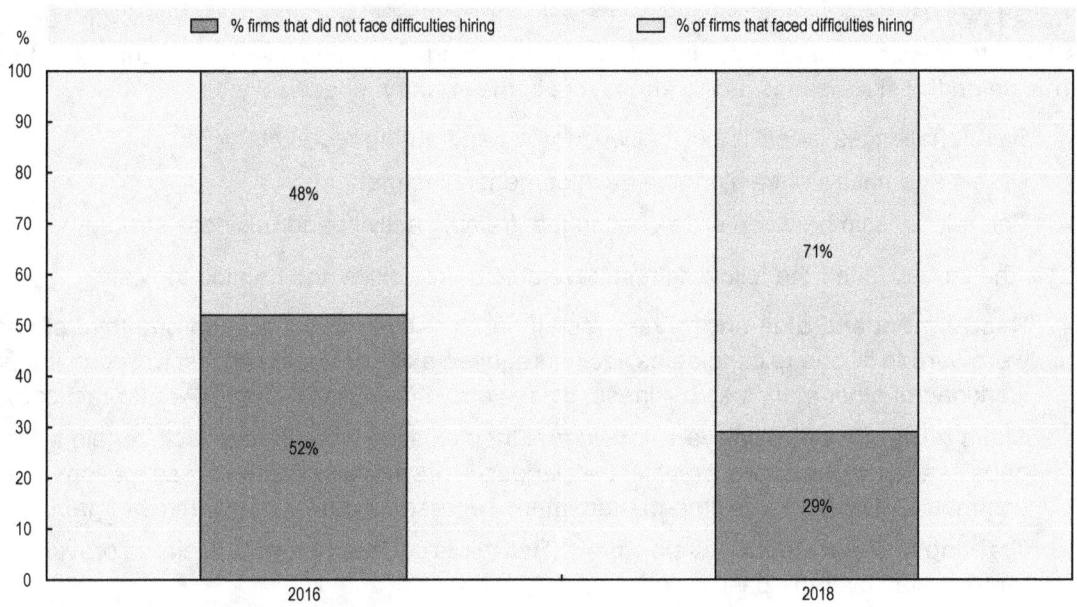

Note: Responses based on responses to Basque employer federation study.
Source: Confebask, Necesidades de empleo u cualificaciones de las empresas vascas para 2018.

Figure 4.7. Firm response suggest job quality is a leading reason for the mismatch

Cause of hiring difficulty according to firm response

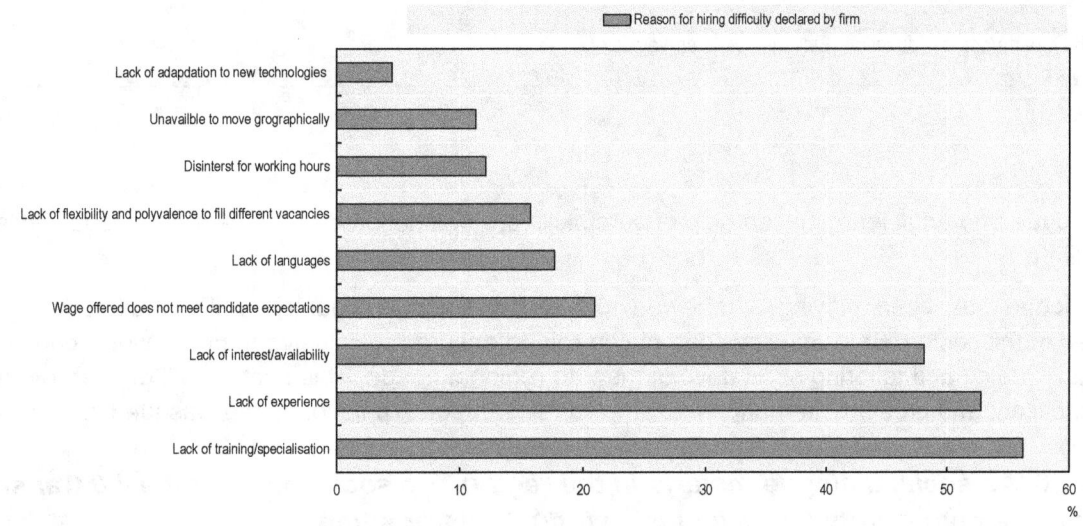

Note: Data based on responses to Basque employer federation study.
Source: Confebask, Necesidades de empleo u cualificaciones de las empresas vascas para 2018.

PREPARING THE BASQUE COUNTRY, SPAIN FOR THE FUTURE OF WORK © OECD 2020

> **Box 4.2. A government employer survey of firms can reinforce information on skills needs and use**
>
> **The UK Department for education administers the UK Employer Skills Survey**
>
> As part of the UK Employer Skills Survey (ESS), the UK Department for Education surveys responses from over 87 000 employers. The ESS is conducted every two years and began in 2011. The survey is conducted by telephone in two parts: a first survey of UK firms, and a second follow-up survey which asks firms to respond at employer investments in training. The objective of the survey is to provide information on the skills issues facing employers in the country, specifically:
>
> - Skills challenges faces in existing workforces and during recruitment;
> - Levels and nature of training and development investment;
> - The relationship between skills challenges, training activity and business strategy.
>
> In 2017, the survey found the following results related to key skills and training topics:
>
> - **Recruitment and skill-shortages:** recruitment has grown, but around one third of vacancies were hard to fill due to candidates' lack of required skills or qualifications. This can increase the workload of other staff, lose business, delays and difficulties to change work practices;
> - **Skills gaps**: 13% of employers considered their existing workforce to lack certain skills. These gaps tended to be more prevalent in labour- and service-intensive occupations. The most common skill lacking was time-management, representing nearly two-thirds of gaps;
> - **Training and workforce development**: Two thirds of UK employers declared providing training for their staff over the past year;
> - **High performance working:** Around 9% of employers are considered to use high performance work practices. Employers that use such practices tend to provide more training to their employees.
>
> The 2017 ESS report identifies four skills challenges facing the country: finding the right workers, optimising and improving existing worker skills, expanding employee training and improving workplace practices.
>
> Source: UK Department for Education, *Employer skills survey 2017*, https://assets.publishing.service.gov.uk/government/uploads/system/uploads/attachment_data/file/746493/ESS_2017_UK_Report_Controlled_v06.00.pdf.

Social dialogue and adult learning can help ensure skills are best tailored to the region's needs, while job quality is lifted

Social dialogue has been playing a renewed role in the Basque Country, while adult learning has progressed in the region. Both practices can play a role to ensure an inclusive future of work, particularly by lifting job quality and tailoring skills development to regional needs. This section will give an overview of both practices, and present international examples relevant for expansion in the Basque Country.

4.1.6. As social dialogue restarts in the region, the social pact for the 4.0 transition is a key opportunity for an inclusive industrial transition

In 2019, the Basque Country re-launched social dialogue through its *Mesa de Diálogo Social*, the region's social dialogue roundtable. Decentralisation has allowed the development of significant social dialogue at the level of Spanish regions. The roundtable is made up two unions, the Unión General de Trabajadores

(UGT) and the Confederación Sindical de Comisiones Obreras (CCOO), as well as Confebask and the Basque government. Eusko Langileen Alkartasuna-Solidaridad de los Trabajadores Vascos (ELA) and Langile Abertzaleen Batzordeak (LAB), the largest unions in the Basque Country, do not participate in this initiative. Through the roundtable, social partners help design public policies through thematic work sessions with the government. The work of the roundtable is meant to complement sectoral and enterprise-level collective bargaining.

In 2019, the *Mesa de Diálogo Social* reached multiple agreements in the areas of equality, employment, training, workplace health and industry. In the field of training, the roundtable agreed that lifelong learning needs to be promoted across sectors and levels, while reinforcing the Basque Country's system of skills recognition (Mesa de Diálogo Social, 2019[11]). In the field of education, meanwhile, the roundtable agreed that the system needs to take into account both student preferences as well as professional opportunities, educational institutions lack resources to fully understand professional paths, students are not fully aware of Vocational Education and Training (VET) opportunities and gender bias persists.

The roundtable's developing pact on the future of work in industry is a particularly innovative approach. The *Pacto Social Vasco para una Transición justa a la Industria 4.0* aims to anticipate the changes entailed by this 4.0 industrial transition, with collaboration and consensus as key ways to agree on mechanisms to accompany workers through the transition (Mesa de Diálogo Social, 2019[11]). Through this pact, employer and worker representatives have been able to express their priorities, with particular attention on anticipating the new skills that will needed from the workforce.

The plan foresees tailored action plans around worker skills, to ensure workers are reskilled without losing their jobs. The Basque government will play a key role in this transition by putting in place specialisation programmes to train workers to respond to the skills needs identified by employers, while Lanbide will take the role of finding employment for those who face redundancies. The government's social affairs department, meanwhile, will support worker incomes through this transition. This pact is a promising example of how social dialogue can anticipate changes in sectors most at risk of automation. To ensure its effectiveness, the Basque government can also assist employers to precisely identify upcoming skills needs, for instance through an employer survey or by supplementing employer analyses with Lanbide's data on the labour market. Moreover, the pact could be a model for agreements on other challenges, such as over-qualification.

4.1.7. Social partners are creating labour market observatories in the Basque Country to raise job quality and better diagnose skills

Labour market observatories can form the basis of new tools to meet the future of work. In particular, the roundtable has agreed to create an Observatorio Vasco de Cultura Preventiva en la Pequeña y Mediana Empresa, or a Basque observatory for risk prevention in SMEs; to gather information on health and occupational safety in the region, formulate a diagnostic report, write specific action plans for sectors or occupations most at risk and for action items to be carried out and monitored by the roundtable (Mesa de Diálogo Social, 2019[11]). Similarly, the roundtable envisages the creation of skill observatory, to evaluate skills needs and to define and formulate job profiles. The roundtable also suggests the creation of a public sector employment observatory to analyse employment evolutions in public administration. These tools could serve as useful ways to carry out fieldwork among employers and workers on the evolving nature of tasks, merging this information with quantitative data available from Lanbide. Across the OECD, social partners are taking similar steps to prepare for the future of work and ensure workers are accompanied through reskilling. In Sweden, for instance, social partners created Job Security Councils, centres that are funded by employer contributions to provide services and guidance to workers who are laid off (Box 4.3). Such councils correspond to the region's tradition of social dialogue, and could constitute a concrete step to ensure those workers who face redundancy due to automation are supported.

> **Box 4.3. In Sweden, Job Security Councils support workers through transition**
>
> **Sector-level agreements created job security councils to support employees through retraining**
>
> Job security councils provide guidance and support into education or employment to workers who have been dismissed collectively. The OECD has suggested job security councils may be one of the leading reasons for Sweden's high rate of re-employment of displaced workers. The councils state that 90% of participating workers find a job, training or education within nine months. One of the key to job council's effectiveness is early and proactive interventions. Councils intervene before workers are laid off, advising companies and workers as companies predict a process of structural change.
>
> Their main interventions with workers include counselling, career planning, job-search assistance, start-up advice and retraining. Job assistance services are also highly individualised, as counsellors consider workers' qualifications, professional interests, concerns and preferences. In 2020, employees losing their jobs received between EUR 2 000 and 3 000 for supportive measures, in addition to unemployment insurance. Councils also have a far reach as all workers in a sector are covered, and not only union members. Support is usually provided for six to eight months, though some agreements involve support that lasts up to five years or until the employee has found a new job.
>
> Job security councils are created through collective bargaining agreements at the sectoral level. The councils are funded through employer contribution, currently 0.3% of payroll, as determined in sectoral agreements. Job councils can also be created in sub-sectors or occupations, involving less comprehensive support but lower payroll contributions. They are owned jointly by employer organisation and unions as a "collective agreement foundation" in Swedish law.
>
> Source: (Eurofound, 2020[12]); (OECD, 2018[13]).

4.1.8. Lifelong learning is an opportunity for firms to help workers adjust skills

Significant progress have been made to build adult training institutions in the Basque Country. Already in 2003, in a key white paper, the Basque Government recognised the need to build stronger adult education institutions, along with a culture of lifelong learning, to face labour market evolutions (Gobierno Vasco, 2003[14]). Data from the OECD's PIACC survey suggests 45.5% of adults between 25 and 64 years old participate in adult learning in the region, slightly below both Spanish and OECD averages (Figure 4.8). In Spain, 46.4% of the same group participate in adult learning, while 49.1% participate on average in OECD countries. Meanwhile, in Spanish regions such as Catalonia and Madrid, 55% and 48.2% of adults respectively participated in adult learning, higher than the share in the Basque Country. Given the region's high degree of skills mismatch, deepening adult learning could be a key strategy to help employers invest and adjust worker skills as they progress in a company and market demand evolves. Regions across the OECD have started such efforts by raising awareness among companies about the benefits of strong workplace innovation strategies, of which adult learning can be a pillar. In Scotland, the government has engaged with the Scottish employer federation to host workshops with academics and practitioners about the benefits and concrete practices to better engage employees (Box 4.4).

Figure 4.8. Adult learning participation is slightly below the Spanish and OECD average

Participation in adult learning

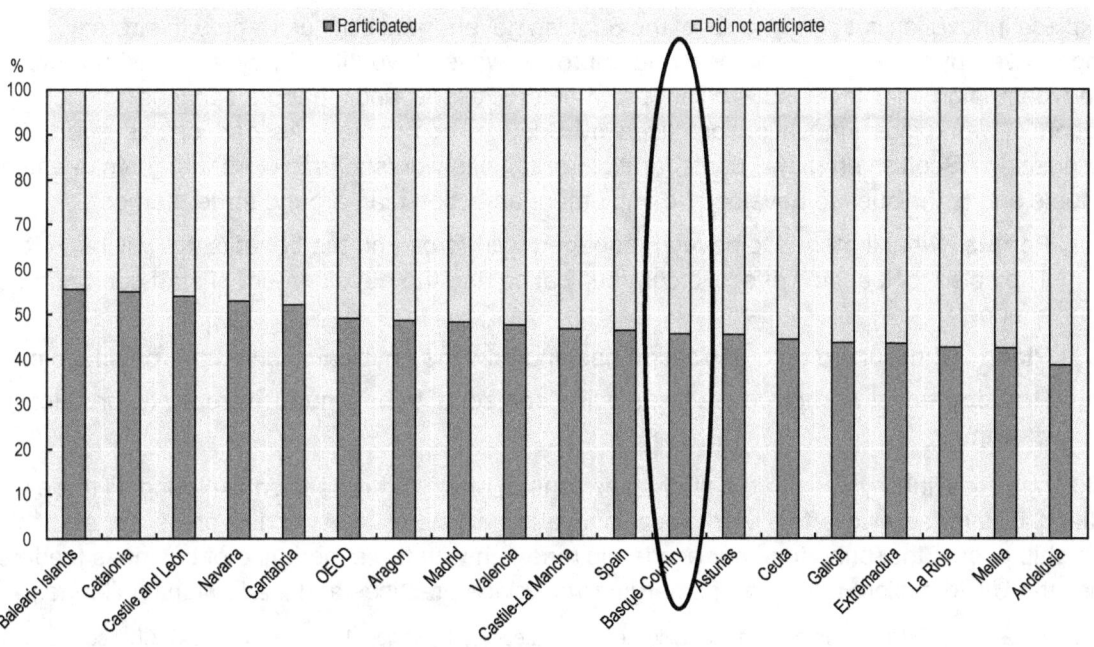

Note: Data includes adults (25-64 years). Numbers for Spain are weighted country averages. Numbers for the OECD are simple averages from the OECD countries included in PIAAC. Data includes people who participated in formal or non-formal training for job-related or non-job related reasonsduring the previous year. Data includes Adult education/ training population (AET) - excludes youths 16-24 in initial cycle of studies (derived).
Source: OECD Survey of Adult Skills (PIAAC).

> **Box 4.4. Workplace innovation in Scotland**
>
> **Developing innovative workplace practices based on staff development**
>
> Workplace innovation is a policy focus of the Scottish government's inclusive growth strategy, it involves change driven by firms to develop new and improved ways of working. They launched an awareness-raising campaign that included workshops, master classes and support services to increase the adoption of workplace innovation practices by Scottish companies. As part of this effort, Scottish Enterprise, the Scottish employer confederation, organises workshops to work with firms to equip them with tools and techniques to develop and implement an action plan around three themes:
>
> - **People** –what it means to have an engaged workforce and the benefits this will bring to a firm. They also look at how effective communication and the development of staff can bring positive change.
> - **Place** –what culture an organisation has and how the physical and virtual workspace can help.
> - **Practice** –what workplace practices a firm can adopt to help nurture creativity, productivity and growth.
>
> Workshops are either run as three half-day sessions or one full-day session exploring all three themes. Scotland Enterprise also offers workplace innovation masterclasses, which are a series of thought leadership events that bring together academic research with the experience of business leaders from across the UK to explore a variety of emerging workplace practices and leadership challenges.
>
> Source: OECD (2020), "Better using skills in the workplace in the Leeds City Region, United Kingdom", OECD Local Economic and Employment Development (LEED) Papers, No. 2020/01, OECD Publishing, Paris, https://doi.org/10.1787/a0e899a0-en.

4.1.9. Firms can modify workplace organisation to reinforce a lifelong learning culture

Lifelong learning can be key for workers to adopt the skills required by employers in the Basque Country. According to an OECD survey, over 25% of survey respondent in the Basque Country indicated workplace responsibilities as the principle barriers to participating in adult learning (Figure 4.9). The high proportion of workers who listed this reason suggests workplace organisation can be an opportunity to increase lifelong learning rates in the region. (Eurofound, 2012[15])In the same survey, 22% of those who responded listed childcare or family responsibilities as leading reasons for not participating in adult learning, while 10.1% listed unexpected events and 8.2% declared the cost as too high. In the same survey, 10.11% listed unexpected events and 8.2% declared the cost as too high. Given the region's experience with inter-firm cooperation, a pertinent international example to reinforce adult learning among companies in the Basque Country can be found in Ireland, where the government has funded learning networks, or groups of companies within the same industry sector or region with similar training needs (Box 4.5).

As in other OECD countries, SMEs struggle to provide the same levels of training as large companies in the Basque Country. Indeed, under 21% of SME employees receive training in the Basque Country, while over 39% of workers in larger firms can benefit from training (Figure 4.10). Large Basque companies may not provide the same level of training as in other parts of Spain, as nearly 56% of employees in large companies in Spain receive training, compared to only around 39% in the Basque Country. Moreover, OECD research has found risk-prevention is also the most common type of training provided by Spanish companies, meaning many firms may be missing the opportunity to provide work-related training (OECD, 2017[16]).

Figure 4.9. Work-place responsibilities are a leading reason for non-participation in adult learning

Barriers to participation in adult learning

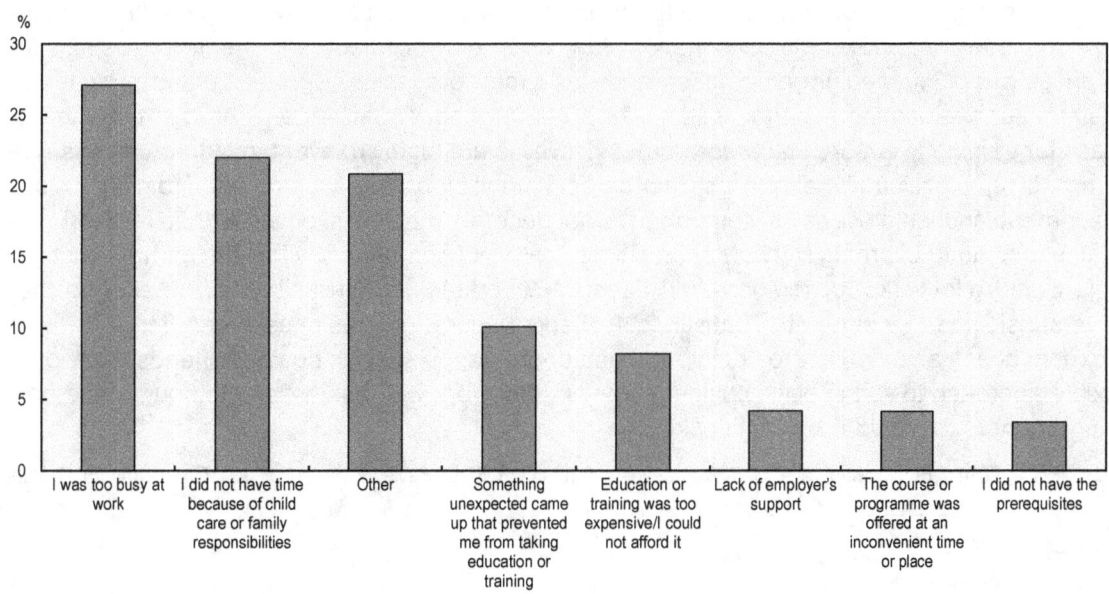

Note: 18+ year olds. Data is based on 79 responses to PIACC survey, representing sample of 261 795 people.
Source: PIAAC (2012, 2015).

Figure 4.10. SMEs tend to train less of their employees than large firms, but large Basque firms fall short of the Spanish average

Coverage rate of employee training

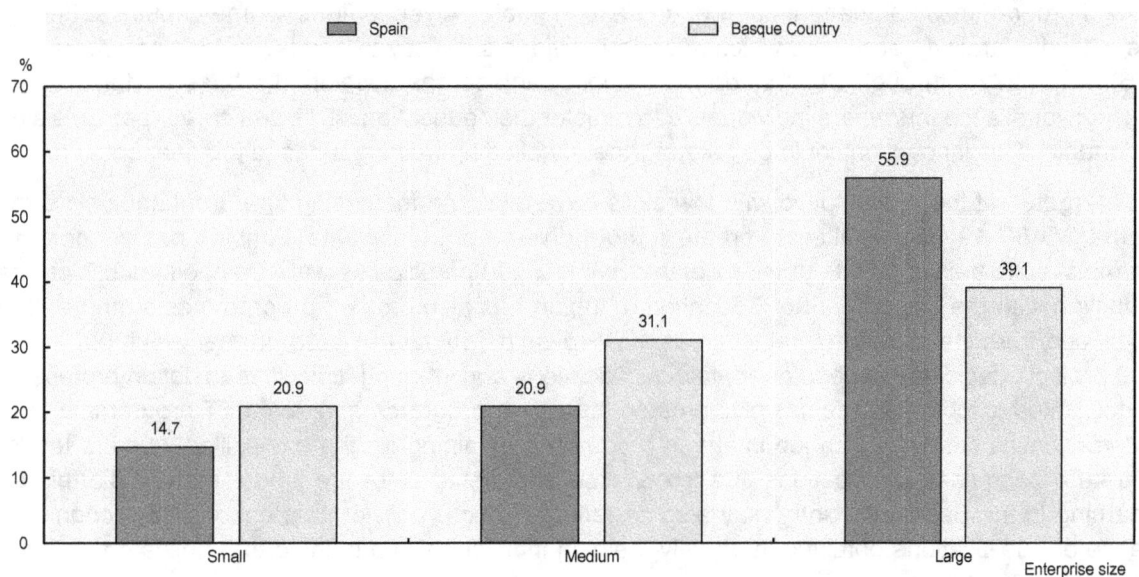

Source: "The Basque Country Competitiveness Report: 2019: Are Skills the Panacea?". Fundae and INE (National Statistics Institute).

> **Box 4.5. Promoting SME networks and enterprise-led learning: The example of Skillnet, Ireland**
>
> Skillnet is a national agency dedicated to the promotion and facilitation of workforce learning in Ireland. It supports over 16 500 companies nationwide, 56% of which are micro-enterprises, 26% small enterprises and 13% medium enterprises and 5% large companies. Skillnet Ireland provides a wide range of valuable learning experiences to over 50 000 trainees. Skillnet encourages firms to lead the process for training to ensure that programmes delivered are highly relevant to industry needs. Training and upskilling significantly enhances the career mobility of the workforce. Training is open to management and employees of companies who become members of a Skillnet Network. Skillnet allocates funding to Learning Networks, which are groups of companies within the same industry sector (Single Sector Networks) or region (Multi Sector Networks) with similar training needs, so they can receive subsidised training. With 70 distinct Networks nationwide, businesses can find a Network that has experience in a particular area of interest and understands specific business needs. Networks offer a flexible approach to suit specific business needs: they work with businesses to source and part-fund training partners to provide relevant upskilling.
>
> Source: OECD (2014), Employment and Skills Strategies in Ireland, OECD Reviews on Local Job Creation, OECD Publishing. http://dx.doi.org/10.1787/9789264207912-en.

4.1.10. Lanbide can become a central actor for a stronger lifelong learning in the Basque Country

Lanbide, partnering with the Education Department and private centres, supports a host of adult training programmes for those struggling most on the labour market. In 2011, the Basque government acquired the responsibility for delivering active labour market policies in the region. In 2017, 1 400 public Vocational Education and Training for Employment (VETE) activities were made available for unemployed people, while over 2 900 were accomplished for those employed (Figure 4.11). Activities are provided for both the unemployed and employed, reaching a coverage rate of 16% for the former, compared to only 3% for the latter. Such programmes can be funded through training quotas given to firms. Some countries, have put in place individual training accounts, which support individuals directly to partake in training programmes (Box 4.6). As of 2020, through *Cuentas de Formación*, Lanbide has developed a base for this policy by creating individual accounts where individuals can register their education, skills and career path in a single online portable. This innovation could be taken further by allotting training funds to job seekers.

Activities targeted at the unemployed with low skills have taken an increasing share of Lanbide's efforts, though the COVID-19 crisis is likely to create a more diverse of participants. Lanbide has supported 20 000 unemployed to train in private training centres, while 3 000 participants were trained in public centres, in conjunction with the Department of Education. Lanbide has also created programmes aimed at those most excluded from the labour market, such as the *Proyectos Singulares* programme, which put in place over 100 projects dedicated to people with few qualifications and learning difficulties to obtain professional certificates linked to jobs. Lanbide has also created the *Hezibi* programme, a dual VET programme, which links apprenticeships directly with job intake in a company. Training for the low-skilled workers tends to concentrate on acquiring certifications or accreditation in order to enter the labour market. To this end, adult learning in the Basque Country may also benefit from more policies that encourage recognition of experience or qualifications obtained informally, helping individuals into training that builds on their skills (Eurofound, 2009[17]).

> ### Box 4.6. Individual training accounts as a response to the future of work
>
> **How are France and Singapore are implementing the right to training**
>
> ***Compte Personnel de Formation, France***
>
> Among individual learning schemes, the French Compte Personnel de Formation (CPF) is frequently cited as an interesting new approach which could boost participation in the new world of work, and the only example of individual learning account in the world. Introduced in 2015 to replace an earlier training account (*Droit Individuel à la Formation*), the CPF is available for all labour force participants and it is financed through a compulsory training levy on firms.
>
> The CPF is a virtual, individual account in which training rights are accumulated over time. It is virtual in the sense that resources are mobilised if training is actually undertaken. As part of the programme, individuals get EUR 500 per year, capped at EUR 5 000 in the standard case, and training programmes are required to deliver a certificate. The CPF has involved 627 205 participants in 2018 or 2.1% of the labour force.
>
> ***SkillsFuture Credit, Singapore***
>
> Introduced in 2016, the SkillsFuture Credit (SFC) consists is a lifetime voucher available to all citizens aged 25 and above, and it is financed through general taxation. Eligible Singaporean citizens receive an opening credit of SGD 500, without time limits, and the government provides periodic top-ups. The credit can be used on top of existing government course subsidies to pay for a wide range of approved skills-related courses, including online courses, subsidised or approved by SkillsFuture Singapore. These include selected courses offered by Ministry of Education-funded institutions, including the Institute of Technical Education, polytechnics, autonomous universities, Singapore University of Social Sciences, LASALLE College of the Arts and Nanyang Academy of Fine Arts. The SkillsFuture Credit has involved 431 000 participants over 2016-18 and 146 000 in 2018, respectively 12% and 4% of the labour force.
>
> Source: OECD (2018), Economic Outlook for Southeast Asia, China and India 2019: Towards Smart UrbanTransportation, OECD Publishing, Paris.https://doi.org/10.1787/saeo-2019-en; SkillsFuture (2019), *SkillsFuture: 2018 Year In Review*, https://www.skillsfuture.sg/NewsAndUpdates/DetailPage/a35eccac-55a5-4f37-bd2f-0e082c6caf70 (accessed on 14 January 2020).

Figure 4.11. Since 2011, Lanbide has developed a volley of VETE programmes to support adult learning in the region

Number of training activities for unemployed versus employed in the Basque Country

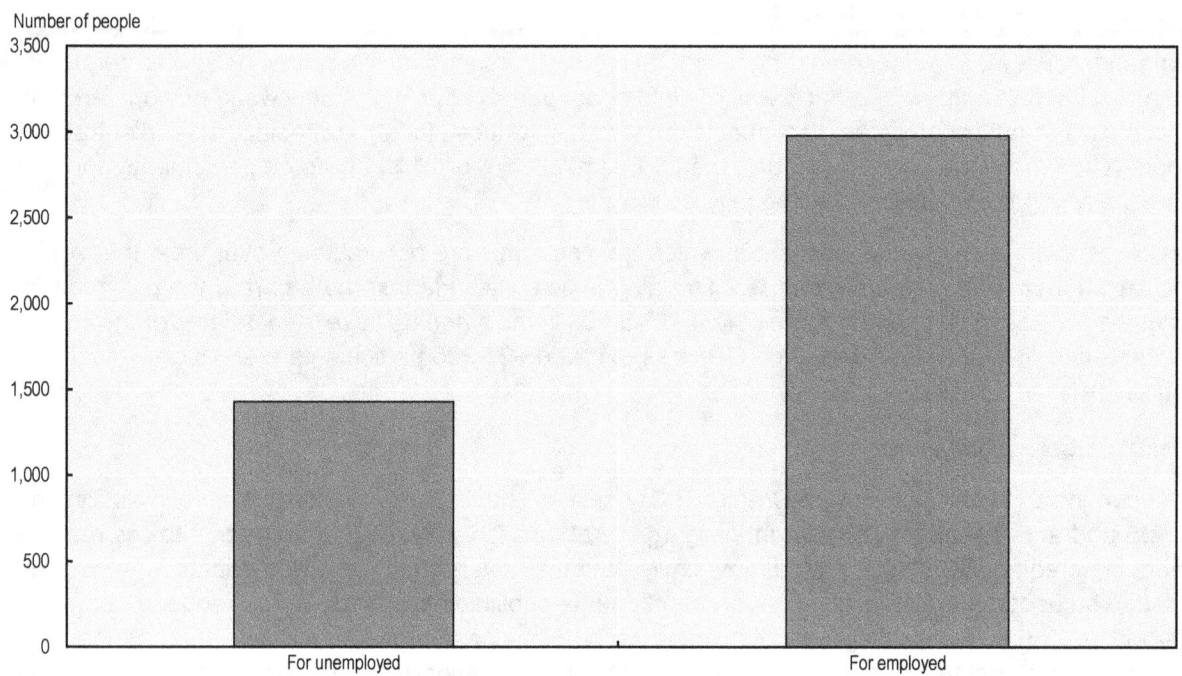

Note: VETE indicators for the unemployed and employed in the Basque Country (carried out in 2017).
Source: "The Basque Country Competitiveness Report: 2019: Are Skills the Panacea?". Orkestra. .

4.2. The Basque Vocation educational and training system

In this sector, the Basque Country's VET system will be presented, highlighting its role as an anchor institution for skills matching. To do so, international examples will be presented from countries that emphasise different elements of training and education (Cedefop, 2017[18]).

4.2.1. VET has gained prominence in the Basque education system

The Basque Country has many prerogatives in Vocational Education and Training (VET), which has allowed VET to develop a central role in the Basque Country. In 1997, a major reform established an integrated training plan that mirrored occupations and monitored the quality of trainings. It also created a network of providers headed by the Basque Institute for Vocational Guidance, the first institute of its kind in Spain. In 2004, the government reformed vocational education to better respond to labour market needs. Between 2011 and 2013, the newly created Basque public employment service, Lanbide, also started taking up an active role in vocational education. Lanbide has been offering training measures, targeted at retraining for those with lower skills. In 2016, governing parties agreed to a volley of changes in VET, including closer ties with firm, a greater emphasis on innovation and entrepreneurship, new types of training, part-time education and more specialised programmes to meet company needs (Gobierno Vasco, 2019[19]). In 2018, the Basque Country passed Law 4/2018 on Vocational Training in the Basque Country, creating the Órgano Superior de Coordinación de la Formación Profesional, a structure that implements the contents of the Training Plan and coordinates among other departments.

The region's fifth Basque Vocational Training Plan is synchronised with the region's employment, education and industrial strategies. The new plan emphasizes the 4.0 context by introducing a greater number of innovative tools, such as smart systems, while facilitating more teaching flexibility. The plan foresees the creation of a Basque Institute for Future Apprenticeships, which will observe job market trends and define professional profiles. The plan also emphasizes a greater number of partnerships and exchanges internationally, and a particular collaboration with the Department of Agriculture, Fishing and Food Policy in order to reflect the region's push in the circular economy, bio-economy, sustainable construction and bio science. The Vocational Training Department, the Basque Vocational Training Board, Tknika, the Basque Institute of Future Apprenticeships, the Basque Institute of Talent in Vocational Training and vocational training centres will carry out different elements of the plan, often in collaboration.

VET has been developed for different skill levels in the region, tailoring training to candidates' prior educational attainment. VET comprises all skills levels to achieve qualification for 170 occupations classified in professional groupings (*familias profesionales*), such as health services or textile industry. The Basque government divides VET into in-school modules, practice modules in training institutes as and short on-the-job parts in real companies. In turn, these modules corresponds to different skill levels. Basic skills level training qualifies young people for helping positions and can be continued with further studies. This basic level is mainly intended for young people between 15 and 17 years of age with compulsory secondary education, and requires the agreement of their parents. The medium skills level builds on the basic one and can be taken by young people above 25 years of age with competitive school and/or basic level training results. The high skills level (*técnico superior*), meanwhile, is meant for students who have passed the medium level or have graduated from a high school or university. It is meant to help students obtain qualification for practicing higher qualified technical work or to enter university studies. Both medium and high-skills level trainings are subject to entry quotas and selections procedures depending on the number of applicants (Inspección General de Educación, 2018[20]).

Training institute teachers drafted training curricula jointly with training mentors in the companies based on the skills needs and the prior knowledge of applicants. The training institute takes on the overall responsibility for the training content and implementation of the curricula. The employer selects the applicants that are pre-selected and proposed by the institute and signs a dual education contract with the applicant (Gobierno Vasco, 2019[21])

VET enrolment has grown as VET institutions have gained a more prominent role in the Basque Country. Between 2011 and 2019, enrolment in VET increased from approximately 34 000 to almost 40 000 people (Figure 4.12). Women still partake less in VET compared to men, having only increased enrolment slightly from approximately 13 000 to 14 000 people. Students have also chosen different sectors for training since 2011. Mechanical work still leads enrolment with over 6 200 students, or 15% of total programme enrolment, reflecting the region's industrial base (Figure 4.13). Some programmes have come to draw more enrolment over time, such as information and communication as well as socio-cultural and community services, which have risen respectively from 5.7% to 8% and 4.5% to 8% of total enrolment. Nonetheless these programmes remain heavily divided by gender, with a large majority of males enrolled in information and communications and females in socio-cultural and community services.

Reforms in professional education have recently unfolded across OECD countries. In France, apprenticeship programmes are being expanded to all skills levels, including tertiary education, while Finland is taking a lifelong approach to VET, including for adults to participate after years of work experience (Box 4.7). The Basque Country could learn from the experiences of OECD countries to expand its successful VET youth programmes to older age cohorts and higher skill levels.

Figure 4.12. VET enrolment has been rising in the Basque Country since 2011, though women make up a small share of students

Evolution of VET enrolment in the Basque Country

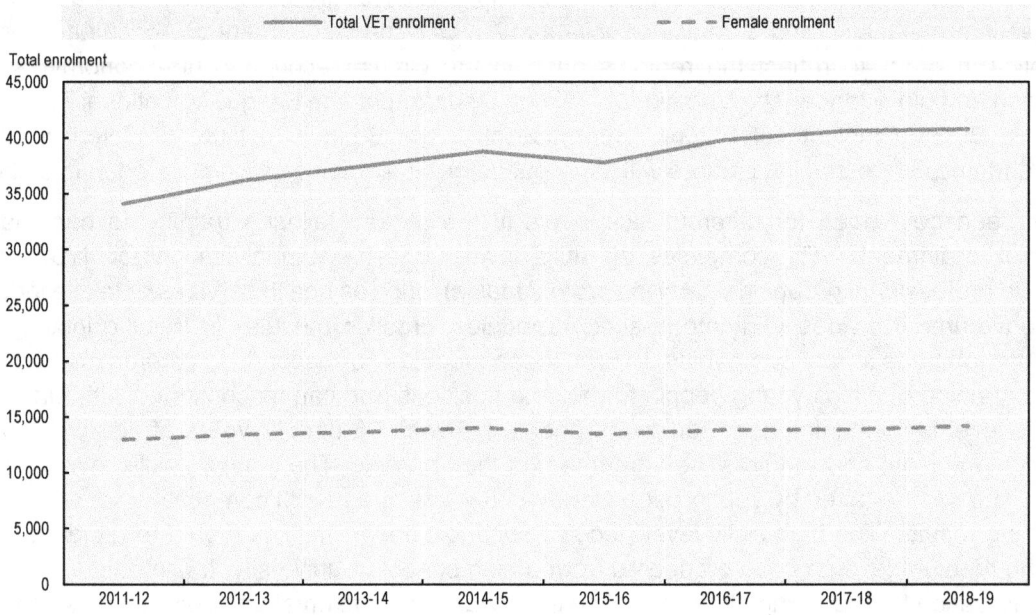

Source: Tknika.

Figure 4.13. Mechanical production and IT and communications led enrolment in 2019

Total enrolment in selected VET sectors, 2011-19

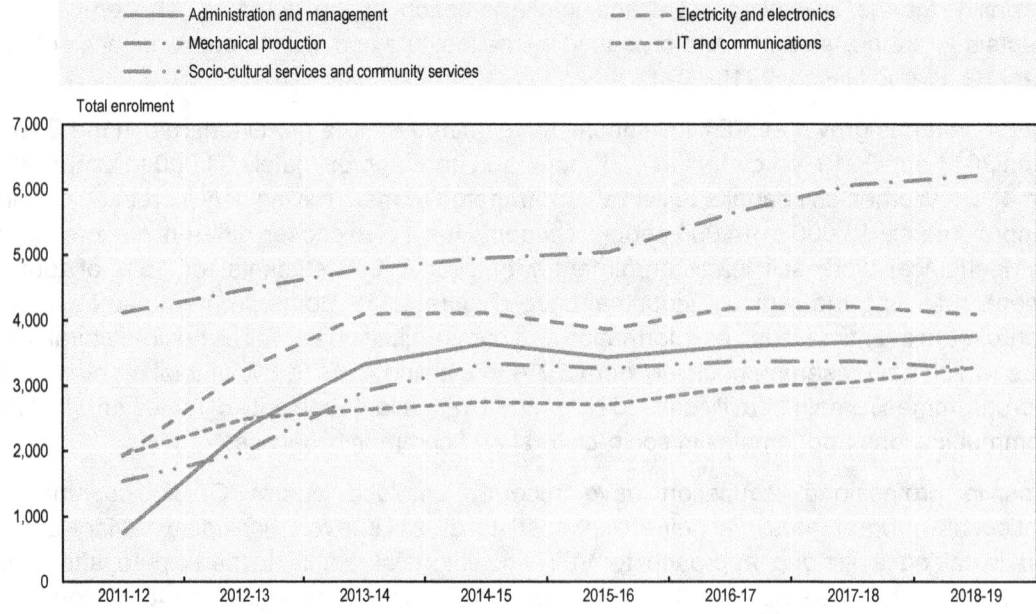

Source: Tknika.

> **Box 4.7. Understanding VET as life-long learning in France and Finland**
>
> France has promoted the idea of apprenticeships from a particular skill level to an arrangement for various skills levels. Moreover, the country is taking the idea of learning on the job combined with schooling as a crosscutting learning approach rather than as one segment of the education system detached from others, as is more typical of academic careers. At the same time, France is more actively validating prior learning in the national qualifications framework. Thus, this process opens a new skills source and makes it visible in the documentation and development of lifelong learning. French law promotes a "lifelong learning VET" that considers education supply for learning approaches, learning sites, and different age groups.
>
> In Finland, VET is an integral part of the education system and centrally managed. Finland distinguishes basic VET and adult VET, connecting learning with job practice. The basic VET for young people is more based on school knowledge than the adult one, but both put vocational skills demonstration at the core. Moreover, they mine talent and experience by opening the possibility for students to show their skills and earn a degree with their ability rather than basing the degree on what they attend in school. Since 1998 all VET graduates have been eligible to access polytechnics and universities in Finland, thus elevating the status of VET in the education system.
>
> Source: Cedefop (2017), The changing nature and role of vocational education and training in Europe Volume 2: results of a survey among European VET experts, https://www.cedefop.europa.eu/files/5564_en.pdf.

4.2.2. Vocational educational levels are high, but automation will change the job market for middle skill occupations

The quality of vocational training in the Basque Country is valued by employers and worker representatives. According to Confebask and CCOO, communication with companies helps design trainings that respond to actual skills demands of the Basque Country (Confebask, 2018[22]). In a recent evaluation of the Basque Employment Plan 2020 commissioned by the Basque Government, increasing dialogue with the firms has been regarded as positive, especially components involving on-the-job training along with classroom teaching. The growing international aspect of trainings, for example through links with the Erasmus+ programme, are also helping extended valuable international experiences to vocational education students (Gobierno Vasco, 2018[23]).

Automation, however, will significantly change many of the middle skill jobs for which the Basque VET system prepares students, requiring VET to adapt and employers to adjust on-work training. The Basque Country has prepared for these changes through multiple efforts. For instance, since its creation in 2004, the Tknika Centre for Applied Innovation in Vocational Training has played the unique role of connecting innovation in companies to training centres (Box 4.8). The *Agenda Digital de Euskadi 2020*, meanwhile, constitutes a wide set of initiatives to accompany the digitalisation of Basque companies. The plan also includes specific initiatives to assist Basque SMEs, particularly those associated with the region's core manufacturing industry, in integrating digital technologies.

OECD countries are also introducing digitalisation strategies at the local level, providing insights for the Basque Country. In Germany, for example, *Aus und Weiterbildung* 4.0 (Vocational education and training 4.0) in the region of Ostbrandenburg, close to Berlin, is run by the German public employment service (Bundesinstitut für Berufsbildung, 2019[24]). The initiative supports small and medium sized enterprises to adapt their training programmes to the digital requirements of the new world of work. The project informs companies on how new technological developments of their sectors can be integrated into their vocational and dual education schemes. It consults companies on individual bases and pilots solutions such as digital applications in training situations and on-the-job training. The initiative also addresses the necessary skills development for trainers and advisors of the employment services who help clients find an apprenticeship. The national development programme that roofs initiatives such as this is funded by the Ministry for Education and Research, with 48 million EUR from the national budget and a co-financing by the European Social Fund of 60 million Euro.

> Box 4.8. Tknika, the Basque Centre for Applied Innovation in Vocational Training
>
> **Innovation through partnership between firms and VET centres**
>
> In 2004, the Basque Government opened *Tknika*, the Basque Centre for Applied Innovation in Vocational Training as part of the *Viceconsejería de Formación Profesional*, or government department dedicated for professional training, in the Basque Department of Education. *Tknika* was founded as a centre to tie training centres with companies, in order to connect innovation with training. As part of the *Fifth Vocational Training Plan 2019-2021* and *Law 4/2018* on professional training in the Basque Country, *Tknika* becomes the "technical body responsible for research and applied innovation and the transfer of the results of R+D+I projects to all the centres that provide vocational training in the Basque Autonomous Community". The plan sets out several roles for *Tknika*:
> - Conduct research in VET innovation;
> - Encouraging relations between innovation and educational actors;
> - Training VET teachers in innovation in production processes, with a focus on new learning environments;
> - Encouraging the internationalisation of VET training in the region;
> - And stimulating entrepreneurship among students.
>
> As such, *Tknika* plays the unique intermediary role between VET centres, universities and research centres and Basque companies. The centre stresses technological innovation in VET centres, with a range of activities from digitisation, connectivity and advanced technologies. *Tknika* also has a particular focus on creating partnerships between training centres and SMEs, as these may not have access to the innovation resources of large companies while also constituting a major employment base. As part of this process, *Tknika* works with SMEs in the region to develop applied innovation projects, guiding them step-by-step through innovation projects.
>
> Source: Gobierno Vasco (2019), V Plan Vasco de Formación Profesional 2019–2021: La Formación Profesional en el entorno de la 4ª Revolución Industrial, http://www.euskadi.eus/contenidos/informacion/fpgeneral/es_def/adjuntos/V-PLAN-FP-CASazk.pdf.

4.2.3. Dual education is gaining traction in the region, expansion to vulnerable groups and university could reinforce its reach

Interest in dual education is growing among students and employers in the Basque Country. Dual education is a set of hybrid training-employment initiatives, most common in Vocational Education and Training (VET), that equip students with demanded skills by companies in real work environments. In the Basque Country, 1 913 apprentices took part in the 2017-2018 cycle, as did 1 122 companies, while 96% of trainees entered employment after graduation. In a recent survey, graduate, employers and training institutions tended to evaluate dual education positively, with market above eight out of ten. (Gobierno Vasco, 2018[23]). The classroom component of dual education allows students to improve their qualifications, while the practical component opens access to employment from a direct contact with companies. Companies who take on apprentices in the dual scheme are also more likely to keep them upon graduation and offer them a longer employment contract. Germany's dual education system, for example, benefits from a regular uptake rate of apprentices of over 95% (Seibert, 2017[25]). In Slovenia, the country helps students develop individualised apprenticeship plans, a helpful policy to help ensure students are supported through their apprenticeship (Box 4.9).

Dual education is anchored in workplace training

Dual education privileges time in the workplace in the Basque Country. Two-year programmes enrich the skills students have acquired in vocational education by offering between 800 and 1 200 hours in companies, while the three-year programme adds over 3 000 hours of working in the company, and approximately 1 500 hours in the classroom. During the first year of the dual education the time spent in the company cannot exceed 75% of the overall training time, while in the second year, it has to be less than 85%. In the region, the *Dual to World* programmes adds one year to the three-year programme, placing apprentices abroad, usually in an international branch or representation of the company in which have been training. Subsidies are also available for dual education, for example for students with disabilities.

Dual education is well-established in middle and high level VET in the Basque Country

Dual education is expanding across sectors and education levels. In the Basque Country, dual VET is available in 20 professional sectors, in which approximately 1 200 students participate each year. Dual training at universities is starting as well, with trials in some degrees such as Engineering in Process and Product Innovation opening 50 spaces in the 2015-2016 school year. Dual VET is currently offered in 97 training centres in the Basque Country. Almost 90% of the more than 41 000 enrolled students in 2019 are being trained in middle or high level skills. More than half of the students qualify for occupations in the service sector, while 45% enter industry.

Dual education can continue to expand in the region, while greater evaluation could also guide development

Instructors, employers and students can all be informed about dual education possibilities in the region to ensure they have equitable access to this policy. In particular, policymakers are considering widening the opportunities and making it easier for small and medium sized enterprises to participate in apprenticeship schemes and find ways to have less- skilled people enter dual education programmes. At the same time, teachers need to be provided with the necessary skills to take advantage of the scheme. Dual education can continue to be expanded to universities, including by considering apprenticeship contracts in masters degrees. Systematic evaluation of the paths of dual education graduates may also help adjust curricula and programming.

> **Box 4.9. Individual, co-drafted apprenticeship plans in Slovenia**
>
> Slovenia has adopted a dual education system based on individual apprenticeship plans that are drafted, agreed and followed-up among representatives of the sector chamber, mentors at the company of work, apprentices and training institutes. The plan describes the rights and responsibilities of each actor in the learning environment and serves as the frame for evaluating the apprentice's performance. The apprenticeship plan is not pre-defined on the state level and can be adjusted as needed by the educational institute, employer or student. It serves more as a commitment and planning tool that guides the individual dual education of each student. Students maintain an apprenticeship diary, where they document their development and self-assess throughout their learning.
>
> The three years of dual education in Slovenia do not contain many evaluations. Of the few, there is a mid-term examination that is done after two years of training, and needs to be passed in order to enter the last year. The chambers coordinate and supervise the dates and contents of the midterm with the employers/mentors and the expert supervisors of the training institutes. In doing so, they follow-up on the agreements taken in the apprenticeship plans. Apart from accuracy, compliance with health and safety regulations and other general knowledge, the midterm explicitly checks how the apprentices transferred the agreements from the apprenticeship plan into their company experience and how closely they have worked with their diary.
>
> Source: Moritsch, S. (2019), *Innovative Training Programmes for Dual Education in the Alpine Space*, https://www.alpine-space.eu/projects/dualplus/pdfs/results/dt231-best-practice-collection-report.pdf.

Conclusion

Educational attainment in the Basque Country has risen significantly in the last 20 years, though the evolution of Basque jobs has not mirrored this trend, as 30% of workers in the region are working in jobs below their qualification level. Evidence suggests skills mismatch and low job quality may be main drivers of over-qualification, including the under-utilisation of skills, wages and contract stability. As part of strong workforce strategies, adult learning and social dialogue has progressed in the region, constituting opportunities for the region. As Vocational Education and Training (VET) has grown in the Basque Country, the region could use dual VET apprenticeships as a way to tighten links between the skill needs of employers and those of the workforce, particularly as technology reshapes many middle skill job.

References

Bundesinstitut für Berufsbildung (2019), *Ausbildung im digitalen Wandel Strategien für kleine und mittlere Unternehmen.* [24]

Cedefop (2017), *The changing nature and role of vocational education and training in Europe Volume 2: results of a survey among European VET experts*, https://www.cedefop.europa.eu/files/5564_en.pdf. [18]

Confebask (2018), *Manual de instructores. Formación professional dual en régimen de alternancia*, http://formacion.confebask.es/Corporativa/Default.aspx?Xqp5O3l6Vf29NpLMKp62346789bTaQ90785678d90785678d. [22]

Eurofound (2020), *Job security councils*, https://www.eurofound.europa.eu/observatories/emcc/erm/support-instrument/job-security-councils. [12]

Eurofound (2012), *Work organisation and innovation*, https://www.eurofound.europa.eu/sites/default/files/ef_publication/field_ef_document/ef1272en.pdf. [15]

Eurofound (2009), *Low-qualified workers in Europe*, https://www.eurofound.europa.eu/sites/default/files/ef_files/docs/ewco/tn0810036s/tn0810036s.pdf. [17]

Fernández-Macías, E. (2012), "Job Polarization in Europe? Changes in the Employment Structure and Job Quality, 1995-2007", *Work and Occupations*, Vol. 39/2, pp. 157-182, https://doi.org/10.1177/0730888411427078. [1]

Gobierno Vasco (2019), *V Plan Vasco de Formación Profesional 2019-2021*, https://www.euskadi.eus/contenidos/informacion/fpgeneral/es_def/adjuntos/V-PLAN-FP-CASazk.pdf. [19]

Gobierno Vasco (2019), *V Plan Vasco de Formación Profesional 2019–2021: La Formación Profesional en el entorno de la 4ª Revolución Industrial*, http://www.euskadi.eus/contenidos/informacion/fpgeneral/es_def/adjuntos/V-PLAN-FP-CASazk.pdf. [21]

Gobierno Vasco (2018), *Evaluación de la puesta en marcha y primera fase de implementación de la Estrategia Vasca de Empleo 2020.* [23]

Gobierno Vasco (2003), *The Basque Country: a learning region*, https://www.euskadi.eus/contenidos/informacion/dia6/en_2027/adjuntos/publications_in_english/libro_blanco_en.pdf. [14]

Inspección General de Educación (2018), *Formación profesional: Exenciones, convalidaciones, equivalencias y homologaciones*, https://www.euskadi.eus/contenidos/informacion/legelabur/es_def/adjuntos/Convalidaciones.Septiembre%202018_def.pdf. [20]

International Federation of Robotics (IFR) (2018), *Executive Summary World Robotics 2018 Industrial Robots*, https://ifr.org/downloads/press2018/Executive_Summary_WR_2018_Industrial_Robots.pdf. [5]

Mesa de Diálogo Social (2019), *Informe de seguimiento y evaluación de la actividad de la mesa de dialogo social durante el año 2019*. [11]

OECD (2019), *Employment Oulook 2019: The Future of Work*, https://doi.org/10.1787/9ee00155-en. [10]

OECD (2018), *Employment Outlook 2018*, OECD Publishing, Paris, http://dx.doi.org/10.1787/empl_outlook-2018-e. [13]

OECD (2017), *Getting Skills Right: Spain*, http://dx.doi.org/10.1787/9789264282346-en. [16]

OECD (2015), *In It Together: Why Less Inequality Benefits All*, OECD Publishing, Paris, http://dx.doi.org/10.1787/9789264235120-en. [26]

OECD/ILO (2017), *Better Use of Skills in the Workplace: Why It Matters for Productivity and Local Jobs*, http://dx.doi.org/10.1787/9789264281394-en. [8]

OECD/ILO (2017), *Better Use of Skills in the Workplace: Why It Matters for Productivity and Local Jobs*, OECD Publishing, Paris, https://dx.doi.org/10.1787/9789264281394-en. [9]

Oesch, D. and J. Rodríguez Menés (2011), "Upgrading or polarization? Occupational change in Britain, Germany, Spain and Switzerland, 1990 – 2008", *Socio-Economic Review*, Vol. 9, pp. 503–531, http://dx.doi.org/0.1093/ser/mwq029. [2]

Orkestra (2019), *El futuro del empleo en la CAPV*. [7]

Peugny, C. (2019), "The decline in middle-skilled employment in 12 European countries: New evidence for job polarisation", *Research and Politics*, Vol. January-March, pp. 1-7, http://dx.doi.org/0.1177/2053168018823131. [3]

Pierson, P. (2001), *Post-Industrial Pressures on the Mature Welfare States*, Oxford University Press. [6]

Sebastian, R. and F. Biagi (2018), *The Routine Biased Technical Change hypothesis: a critical review*, European Commission, Luxembourg, http://dx.doi.org/:10.2760/986914, JRC11317. [4]

Seibert, H. (2017), *Meist gelingt ein nahtloser Übergang*. [25]

www.ingramcontent.com/pod-product-compliance
Lightning Source LLC
Chambersburg PA
CBHW082344220526
45470CB00008B/2638